I0114138

THE CANARY ON THE COUCH

The Psychology
of Jewish Self-
Delusions in the
Face of Rising
Antisemitism

THE CANARY ON THE COUCH

The Psychology
of Jewish Self-
Delusions in the
Face of Rising
Antisemitism

**Dr. Kenneth
Levin**

ACADEMIC STUDIES PRESS

BOSTON

2025

Print LCCN 2025027721

Copyright © 2025, Kenneth Levin, author

ISBN 9798897830398 (hardback)
ISBN 9798897830404 (Adobe PDF)
ISBN 9798897830411 (ePub)

Book design by Lapiz Digital Services
Cover design by Ivan Grave

Published by Academic Studies Press
1007 Chestnut Street
Newton, MA 02464, USA
press@academicstudiespress.com
www.academicstudiespress.com

Some passages in the present work previously appeared in the author's earlier book
The Oslo Syndrome: Delusions of a People Under Siege (Smith and Kraus Global, 2005).

To those who honorably sought to defend a vital asset
for Israel and the Jewish people:
Richard Allen, Alan Altman, Linda Frieze, Richard Rubin, Robert Weisberg

Contents

Chapter One

The Problem

———

"It's all about the Benjamins baby."

> Ilhan Omar, asserting that Congressional support for
> Israel is based on Jewish payoffs; February 10, 2019

"I want to talk about the political influence in this country that says it's OK to push for allegiance to a foreign country [Israel]."

> Ilhan Omar, accusing American Jews of dual loyalty; February 2019

"Omar Holding Secret Fundraisers with Islamic Groups Tied to Terror"

> Adam Kredo, *Washington Free Beacon*, March 23, 2019

"Why is the Reform Movement Defending an Antisemite?"

> Benjamin Kerstein, *Jewish News Syndicate*, January 23, 2023

It has often been said (so often as to become trite to some) that the Jews are the miners' canary of Western civilization. That is, like canaries taken into the shafts by coal miners for the purpose of signaling—should they suddenly expire—the presence of poisonous fumes, attacks on Jews are an early sign of some social and political toxin that inevitably threatens the wider population as well. And there is certainly much evidence in the history of the West to support the metaphor.

The metaphor is invoked most when social and political conditions such as extensive economic hardship, extreme political polarization, and widespread sense of vulnerability to dangerous, hostile forces prevail; the very conditions under which the targeting of the Jews is particularly likely to flourish. Not surprisingly, at such times significant segments of the broader society are inclined to be at best unreceptive and indifferent to the metaphor's message. What is more surprising is the degree to which the Jews themselves very often fail to recognize the extent of the threats posed by the poisons to which they are exposed, even when those poisons are quite obvious in their expression as Jew-hatred.

The Psychology of Communal Self-Delusion in Response to Threats

One element of this self-defeating response to grave threats is simply the widely common impulse to deny the danger and avert one's gaze. The head-in-the-sand impulse can be found to varying degrees among all groups under serious threat. One might imagine, given the Jews' recurrent experience of ominous situations becoming murderous and even genocidal, that Jews might be more inoculated by communal history against predilections to such denial. But that history has had, for many, the opposite effect. The awareness at some level of the horrors that can transpire reinforces an impulse, however maladaptive, to ignore the reality and engage in wishful thinking.

A potential counterweight to such impulses, a force that can rally the community against such self-destructive responses, is a communal leadership that itself recognizes the dangers facing its members and has the integrity and moral fortitude, and also the respect of the community, sufficient to win its members to more realistic and constructive strategies in response to threats. But in the context of the dramatic recent rise of antisemitism in America, the American Jewish community has, in general, been alarmingly lacking in such leadership.

Denial of danger is found to occur within virtually all populations. But other, related, maladaptive reactions are more particularly characteristic of chronically besieged groups, whether minorities denigrated and marginalized by the surrounding majority or citizens of small states under chronic threat from larger, hostile neighbors. Almost invariably, elements within such threatened groups will embrace the attacks on their community as valid and blame others in the community as being responsible for the assaults. They may then advocate communal reform to placate the besiegers. Or they may seek to escape the community to extricate themselves from the communal taint and spare themselves the negative consequences of being part of the community. Or they may even join the attackers, seeking—by identifying so explicitly with them—to protect themselves even more definitively from being a victim of the siege.

The common denominator among those who choose to attribute responsibility for the siege to other members of the victimized community, who rationalize the calumnies leveled by the haters, is a desire to exercise some control over a situation in which they typically have little or no control. Thus, for example, the subtext of the advocacy of communal reform as a way of addressing the besiegers' indictments—the most common and significant of the three responses noted above—is the wish to believe that proper reforms will inevitably win relief from the siege. There is, however, virtually nothing in the history of such circumstances that support that fantasy.

The paradigmatic model for such a reaction to abuse on the level of individual psychology is found in chronically abused children, especially younger ones. Psychiatrists, psychologists, and social workers doing therapy with such children almost invariably encounter them blaming themselves for the abuse to which they are subjected. Many suggest that the explanation for this lies in the abusers, typically parents or parental surrogates in the case of chronic abuse, conveying to the children that they are "bad," and the children, in their naivete, accepting this at face value. But children are not that naive. They know when they are being victimized.

An alternative, commonly invoked clinical explanation is construing the self-blame as a reflection of children's narcissism. Children are inclined to see themselves as the center of their world and to ascribe to themselves grandiose powers. This, it is argued, predisposes them to assume responsibility for whatever befalls them, good or ill.

But consideration of abused children's existential predicament points to a more incisive explanation for their self-blame. Having typically no means of escape, often barely capable of even imagining escape, they can either resign themselves to being trapped in a horrible situation over which they have no control or they can embrace fantasies of control. They can repress awareness of their victimhood, convince themselves that they are indeed "bad," and endure the pain of that self-comprehension but nurture the fantasy that if they only become "good" their parents will respond positively and the abuse will end. Children almost invariably choose the fantasy of having some control over the reality of having none. In the face of dire circumstances, they give priority to seeking agency and avoiding hopelessness, and adults in comparable circumstances typically do the same.[1]

On the communal level, the response of self-indictment and promotion of self-reform can be seen at times even within ostensibly powerful and secure populations under conditions that entail ongoing threat and vulnerability.

---

1   The professional literature seeking to explain in psychological terms the predilections of victims to embrace the indictments and calumnies of their abusers has often invoked the psychoanalytic concept of "identification with the aggressor." The concept, and the term, were introduced by Anna Freud in the 1930s. (Anna Freud, *The Ego and the Mechanisms of Defense* [Madison, CT: International Universities Press, 1966], especially 109–121.) They have been used to refer to a defense mechanism in which the individual blunts the pain of negative interactions with others, such as criticism or rejection, by embracing the indictment, making it one's own self-criticism. The individual thereby at least attains a sense of being in control of the indictment rather than simply feeling the passive victim of assault by others, and attains also a sense of shared comprehension and rapport with the attacking other rather than feeling simply the targeted outsider.

"Stockholm Syndrome" is another term that has become prominent in recent decades in both professional and popular discussions of people's embrace of the perspectives of their abusers. It largely parallels in its meaning "identification with the aggressor." The term had its origin in an attempted bank robbery in the Swedish capital in 1973 that went awry, with several people being held captive by the would-be robbers for six days in the bank's vault. The captives emerged displaying notable empathy for, and emotional bonding with, their captors. Anna Freud saw identification with the aggressor as, to some degree, a universally employed defense. She found its paradigmatic expression in a universal childhood response to parental criticism. In fact, she saw the child's inclination to embrace at least in part any parental criticism—in order to lessen the pain of the parental attack and to feel more connected to parents—as the foundation of development of the child's conscience, or super-ego. The more particular phenomenon being examined here, the embrace by at least some members of abused groups of the indictments of their abusers, can, again, be most usefully illuminated by considering a more particular developmental paradigm: the predicament, and psychological responses, of children subjected to chronic abuse. The self-indicting response widely recognized and studied in children victimized by early abuse and related traumas is more intense and pervasive than Anna Freud's universal childhood identification with parental criticisms.

It can be argued that, in general, children's profound investment in fantasies of winning desired responses from parents underlies their predisposition to take to heart parental criticism and sustains children's grandiosity, their wish-driven faith in their own powers to transform their situation. (See, for example, Kenneth Levin, *Unconscious Fantasy in Psychotherapy* [Northvale, NJ: Jason Aronson], 1993.) It is this factor amplified by circumstances of abuse that underlies the more extreme and more pervasive self-indictments and concomitant grandiosity of abused children.

One could see it, for example, in trends in the United States in the wake of the terror attacks of September 11, 2001. Those who perpetrated the carnage, as well as their supporters, conveyed in word and deed their grievances against America and their objectives. They declared their deadly hostility not only to America's military and diplomatic presence in the Muslim world but to its cultural presence as well. They proclaimed their determination to pursue a militant path in order to recreate an Islamic caliphate cleansed of all Western "pollution" and to fight for imposition of their Islamic rule worldwide. They asserted that to do so was their religious duty. They made clear that their war against America was predicated on their perception of America as the chief obstacle to their aspirations; and they demonstrated that there were no constraints on the methods and weapons they were prepared to use.

Much of the American public recognized the gravity of the challenge. But there were also many in the country who sought to recast the threat, to rationalize it as a response to American provocations, and to urge policies of self-reform aimed at appeasing the terrorists and their supporters in the delusional hope of thereby extricating the nation from the dangers it faced.

Still, it is particularly among the chronically besieged—minorities subject to abuse and, again, citizens of small states under chronic threat—that one most finds predilections to self-indictment and concomitant pursuit of self-reform in the quest for acceptance and relief from abuse. With the recent recrudescence of antisemitism, some Jews not given to such self-delusions and self-defeating strategies look on those who embrace them as carriers of a uniquely Jewish psychopathology. But, in fact, biographical, autobiographical, sociological, and historical writings touching on other communities living under conditions of chronic duress of one form or another reveal them manifesting similar psychological responses. Additional evidence is provided by sociological and psychological literature addressing prejudice and its ravages more generally. If the propensity for such maladaptive psychological responses has been particularly marked among Jews, its being so is a product of the Jews' particularly long history of oppression, slaughter, and dislocation.

Maladaptive Jewish Responses to the Present Danger

In the context of the recent burgeoning of antisemitism in America, the problematic self-defeating responses of major elements of the Jewish community have not been a significant factor vis-à-vis all sources of the increased

Jew-hatred. In particular, the community has generally been united in calling out antisemitism coming from white supremacist and neo-Nazi sources. But with regard to the hatred emanating from other segments of the population, maladaptive, failing responses, variations on self-blame, and the pursuit of self-reform to accommodate the haters have dominated the reaction of substantial portions of the community and, even more so, major cadres of the communal leadership.

A central theme in the current wave of American antisemitism is that of white privilege and the supposed nefarious place of Jews as beneficiaries of white privilege; indeed, exceptional beneficiaries given their exceptional success in America. In addition, since Jews are privileged by what is characterized as America's racist system, any complaints of bias against them need not be taken seriously. On the contrary, they can be dismissed as insignificant compared to "genuine" bias. Anti-Jewish sentiment is in this way ineluctably tied to the concept of white privilege as it is elaborated upon in many forums of public discourse.

Promotion of Critical Race Theory (CRT) in academia and beyond, and of Diversity, Equity, and Inclusion (DEI) as the action plan for addressing white privilege, has become entrenched throughout both private and public sectors of the American workplace. Intrinsic to Critical Race Theory, and even more explicitly to Diversity, Equity, and Inclusion, is the comprehension of success, whether measured in terms of wealth, achievement, or some other metric, as a zero-sum game. If some racial or ethnic or religious segment of the population is more successful or less successful, it is because the system is unfair, and those who have done better have done so at the expense of others. These CRT and DEI formulas are, obviously, very close to socialist and communist formulations. And, as with the latter, they are predisposed to targeting Jews as deplorable capitalists unfairly benefitting from a corrupt system. This is often stated explicitly, even in school curricula.

The CRT-linked concept of intersectionality holds that all "people of color" have in common being victims of white privilege. A particularly popular sub-theme of intersectionality has been the bizarre notion that Israel is a white colonialist entity victimizing Palestinian "people of color." American Jews are also demonized in this context, for being supporters of Israel.

This avenue of attack on Jews and Israel has resuscitated and amplified Soviet-era indictments of the Jewish state and its Jewish supporters (elaborated by the Soviet Union largely in response to Israel's growing strategic ties with America after the 1967 war). Those attacks, long picked up and parroted by the Far Left in America, characterize Israel as a colonial entity created and backed by Western imperialism.[2]

The response of some within the Jewish community to the white privilege indictment is to embrace it. Among those who do so are people who feel guilty for themselves being beneficiaries of white privilege and feel obliged to make amends. Many more join the attackers in seeing the Jewish community writ large as particular beneficiaries. An example of both phenomena is an article by Rabbi Jonah Dov Pesner that appeared in the *Washington Post* on October 11, 2016, under the title, "As Jews Atone for Yom Kippur, We Need to Confront Our White Privilege." Rabbi Pesner writes, "This year, when I search my soul, I'll be focused on confronting my white privilege." And he urges others to do the same.

Interestingly, Rabbi Pesner notes in his article that he works at the Religious Action Center for Reform Judaism and that he is gratified by the fact that in his workplace there is a conference room where decades earlier people met, "black and white, Christian and Jewish," and drafted significant parts of what became the Civil Rights Act of 1964 and the Voting Rights Act of 1965. What he fails to note is that the aspiration of those people was for a society where all had equal opportunity to achieve; where color, faith, or ethnicity was no obstacle to competing on a level playing field. It was the aspiration and vision of, perhaps most notably, Martin Luther King, Jr.; a vision that is the polar opposite of CRT and DEI, where virtue is measured by equality of outcome. But the morality of the day has changed, and, if that morality indicts Jews in particular, then Rabbi Pesner feels compelled to atone and to urge other Jews to do the same. It is a variation on the abused child's interpreting his inferences of what would appease his abusers as having some transcendent moral significance.

A similarly instructive example is provided by Henry Louis Gates, Jr., university professor and director of the Center for African and African American Research at Harvard. In a *Baltimore Sun* article of July 22, 1992, entitled "The New Black Anti-Semitism is Top-Down and Dangerous," and in a variation of the piece in the *New York Times* of July 20, entitled "Black Demagogues and Pseudo-Scholars," Gates wrote of how a recent survey had shown that Blacks

---

2   On the Soviet origins of the characterization of Israel as an imperialist, colonialist enterprise, see, for example, Izabella Tabarovsky, "Zombie Anti-Zionism," *Tablet Magazine*, July 30, 2024. Tabarovsky writes, "What is so interesting about this half-century-old Soviet propaganda is how precisely it mirrors the language emanating from the anti-Israel left since October 7."

were twice as likely as Whites to hold antisemitic views. He attributes this to the influence of Black radical groups like the Nation of Islam that promote Jew-hatred, as in the antisemitic diatribes of Louis Farrakhan. He writes, in particular, of the Nation of Islam's promoting the lie that Jews dominated the slave trade, and he points out that the references in the Nation of Islam's own text on the subject, *The Secret Relationship*, refute the claim. He notes that Jews, in fact, accounted for less than two percent of the slave trade. He also points out that, in addition to trumpeting this lie, the Nation of Islam argues as well that all Jews today have inherited a special guilt for slavery and that the essential nature of Jews is evil.

"How does this theology of guilt surface in our every day moral discourse?" Gates asks.

> In New York earlier this spring, a forum was held . . . to provide an occasion for blacks and Jews to engage in a dialogue on such issues as slavery and social injustice. Both Jewish and black panelists found common ground, and common causes. But a tone-setting contingent of blacks in the audience took strong issue with the proceedings. Outraged, they demanded to know why the Jews, those historic malefactors, had not apologized to the "descendants of African kings and queens." [. . .] And so the organizer of the event . . . did. Her voice quavering with emotion, she said: "I think I speak for a lot in this room when I say 'I'm sorry.' We're ashamed of it. We hate it . . ."

Why, Gates asks, should this organizer, "whose ancestors survived pogroms and, latterly, the holocaust," be the primary object of such Black wrath? It is a question he answers mainly elsewhere in the article, an answer that will be taken up in a later chapter. But what is notable here is that, in the face of an antisemitic attack, the organizer felt the need to apologize. (Gates indicates that the attackers, unsurprisingly, were not appeased by her mea culpa.) Even though there were other Blacks in the audience who, like Gates, were almost certainly appalled by the attack, Blacks who had found common ground with Jews in the panel discussions, she felt obliged to apologize to the haters.

Beyond Jews who take to heart indictments related to "white privilege," or those attacks stemming directly from Black antisemitism as in Gates's example, still more Jews, including many within the Jewish leadership, embrace the indictments of Israel. They urge Israeli reform to fix the problems with the Palestinians and thereby mollify the Jewish state's critics and those who attack American Jews supposedly for their support of Israel.

An example of this mindset is captured in the writings of Gary Rosenblatt, former editor and publisher of the *New York Jewish Week*, a paper subsidized by the New York Jewish community federation. In an article entitled "Frustration with Israel is Growing Here at Home,"[3] Rosenblatt reports grievances against Israel that he says he has heard from members of the Jewish community, including leaders. Seemingly topping the list, and reflecting a view shared by Rosenblatt, is "The hard fact . . . that Israel's leadership is moving in a direction at odds with the next generation of Americans, including many Jews, who want to see greater efforts to resolve the Palestinian conflict and who put the onus for the impasse on Jerusalem."

In the same vein, he observes, "Whether or not it is fair, the strong perception today is that the Israeli government is moving further right, and intransigent." And "One national leader told me he'd like to fly to Israel, with a group of his top colleagues, to try to convince Netanyahu [who was then prime minister] in dramatic fashion of the need for 'a plan, any plan' to break the impasse." And while these statements are couched as representing what Rosenblatt has heard from others, it is in his own voice that he states near the end of the piece, "Netanyahu and his government will continue to make decisions based on their own narrow and immediate political interests, and we can only hope they will coincide with national interests as well." The obvious implication is that Rosenblatt does not see the prime minister as acting in Israel's national interest, and that—reflecting the thrust of the article—this charge refers specifically to the prime minister's not being forthcoming enough in the quest for peace.

But, in fact, the falling away from Israel among some in the Jewish community, including its leadership, is much less a reaction to Israeli policy than a function of those American Jewish circles wanting to ameliorate anti-Jewish hostility in America. They see attacks on Israel in America, choose to interpret anti-Jewish sentiment as derived from anti-Israel sentiment, and want to believe that sufficient Israeli reform would go far to resolving Jew-hatred.

In the current climate of increased antisemitism, some American critics of Israel actually call for the dismantling of the Jewish state as the proper

---

3   Gary Rosenblatt, "Frustration with Israel is Growing Here at Home," *The New York Jewish Week*, January 6, 2016.

denouement for the allegedly colonialist Zionist project. And there are Jews who embrace this goal as well to address the anti-Jewish hostility supposedly generated by Israel's existence. Notable among such Jews are those affiliated with Jewish Voice for Peace, which essentially advocates the peace of the dead for Israelis.

There are, of course, many members of the Jewish community who recognize, at least to some degree, the unfairness of the various indictments of American Jews and of Israel. But a common response, even among communal leaders, is not to challenge the indictments but rather to downplay them and to accommodate them. Underlying their doing so are variations on the theme of seeking to be "good" to appease the Jews' indicters.

One sees, for example, the emphasis by some on "social justice," which is often invoked to rationalize downplaying and accommodating anti-Jewish attacks. It does so by asserting, in effect, that the attackers are acting on behalf of those who have been society's genuine victims. Therefore, it is a Jewish interest to acknowledge that victimhood, downplay the anti-Jewish assault, and support the "social justice" of seeking redress.

The Jewish Council for Public Affairs (JCPA) has long been the umbrella group for local Jewish Community Relations Councils across the country. Its mandate, and that of the local councils, has been to lead Jewish communal outreach to the wider society with a particular emphasis on promoting social justice. In 2020, the JCPA, along with many local JCRCs, signed a full-page ad in the *New York Times* supporting the Black Lives Matter movement, even though major figures and chapters within the movement had adopted and pursued anti-Jewish and anti-Israel positions and actions. In response to criticism from some quarters of the Jewish community, the JCPA asserted, in essence, that its action was consistent with its role of advocating for social justice.[4]

The Reform movement's defense of serial spewer of antisemitic tropes Ilhan Omar, referenced at the top of the chapter, seems to have reflected a similar weighing of priorities. The support for Omar appeared in a letter signed by six American Jewish groups attacking House Speaker Kevin McCarthy's plan to remove Omar from the House Foreign Affairs Committee. The signers insisted that McCarthy's intent was based on "false accusations that she is

---

4   See, for example, Ron Kampeas, "Seeking Latitude to Press Liberal Causes, the Jewish Council for Public Affairs Distances Itself from Federations," Jewish Telegraphic Agency, December 19, 2022.

antisemitic or anti-Israel." Among the groups advancing this grossly dishon-est whitewashing of Omar and her dangerous promotion of Jew-hatred was the Religious Action Center for Reform Judaism, whose website at one point characterizes its objective as bringing about "a world filled with justice, com-passion and wholeness." To that end, and reflective of its priorities vis-à-vis Jew-hatred, it has not only defended Omar but has in the past, for example, honored the late South African Bishop Desmond Tutu, likewise notorious for a long history of promoting Jew-hatred.[5]

Another, closely aligned, variation of choosing to be "good" to assuage the anti-Jewish attackers rather than challenging them, is the tack of insisting that there remain many common interests with the attackers and that those interests outweigh the threats posed by the anti-Jewish canards. For exam-ple, in June 2022, the North Carolina Democrat Party passed two lie-filled antisemitic and antizionist resolutions, resolutions parroting both Islamist and neo-Nazi propaganda. The state's Jewish Democrats organization would not prioritize the removal of the resolutions because, as the provisional chair of the North Carolina Jewish Democrats opined, to do so would distract from supposedly weightier issues. He is quoted as saying, "We believe these internal party arguments are distracting and do not allow us to focus on such alarming events as the elimination of women's control of their bodies."[6]

All of the responses noted above to the increased antisemitic onslaught in America entail Jews either embracing the indictments of the haters, or essentially ignoring or otherwise downplaying the hatemongering. All are attempts to assuage or otherwise accommodate the haters. Yet all the responses are typically rationalized not as seeking to placate antisemites but rather as holding to a higher morality. This is true of those who internalize the "white privilege" indictments and the attacks on Israel, as well as those who insist that pursuit of "social justice" trumps confronting antisemitism, or those like North Carolina's Jewish Democrats who prioritize supposedly weightier issues.

Those who adopt these reactions to the current antisemitic wave are doing nothing, of course, to break that wave. Yet they believe they are responding to present challenges in manners appropriate to those challenges. In fact, their

---

5   Benjamin Kerstein, "Why is the Reform Movement Defending an Antisemite?" Jewish News Syndicate, January 23, 2023.

6   See Josh Ravitch and Amy Rosenthal, "Jewish Leaders in North Carolina Betray Jewish Interests," Jewish News Syndicate, August 29, 2022.

responses have a long and painful pedigree. Again and again in Jewish history, elements of the community have embraced such reactions in the delusional hope of thereby winning relief from attack. Instead, by failing to acknowledge and answer more realistically the threats confronting them, and by undermining those in the community prepared to respond more appropriately, they have all too often contributed to their communities being left more vulnerable to abuse and attack and have turned difficult situations into yet more difficult ones.

The following chapters will elaborate further on the psychological foundations of these self-deluding and self-defeating strategies. They will also trace their historical foundations, their emergence and evolution over the course of Jewish history, and the often dire consequences that have flowed from them. The last chapter will address what can be done to promote more reality-based and promising responses to the threats currently facing the American Jewish community.

Chapter Two

The Present Antisemitic Onslaught in America

"Cynthia McKinney, a former US congresswoman and 2008 presidential nominee for the Green Party, on Monday promoted a livestream event featuring notorious white supremacist David Duke and the black nationalist author of a book called *Jews Are the Problem*.

"'I know where I'll be and what I'll be watching at 6:00 pm EASTERN time today!' McKinney posted on X . . . Her post included a promotional image of an event with the question, 'Can Black people and White people work together to defeat our common enemy?' written above a large Star of David and a photo of the Sept. 11, 2001, terrorist attacks against the US."[1]

The purveyors of recent antisemitism in the West come from three main groups: the Far Right, the Far Left, and the Islamist segments of Muslim communities in Europe and the United States. In America there is the additional source of Black radicalism.

The massive immigration of Muslims from the Middle East and North Africa into Europe, many bringing with them the hatred of Israel and of Jews

---

1   Andrew Bernard, "'Jews Are the Problem,': Former US Congresswoman Promotes Antisemitic-Black Nationalist Crossover Event," *Algemeiner*, September 11, 2023.

that is typically a staple of the education systems, religious teachings, and government propaganda in their native lands, has created a subpopulation in most of Central and Western Europe in which open, publicly expressed antisemitism is a norm. (Polls of opinion in Muslim states often yield levels of anti-Jewish bias close to 100%. In Muslim countries not even involved in the conflict with Israel, a Pew poll still found very high levels of such bias; for example, in Turkey, at 73%, Pakistan, 78%, and Indonesia, 74%.)[2] The general failure of European governments to critique and address this phenomenon, the failure often even to acknowledge it, has further contributed to rendering it normal. Not even acts of violence against Jews, including murder, at the hands of members of these communities spurred by indoctrinated Jew-hatred have moved governments to acknowledge and address the issue. In France, for example, among a number of gruesome murders of Jews committed by Muslims apparently driven by their bigotry, at least one went essentially unprosecuted and unpunished.

The Right in Europe has generally opposed the mass influx of Muslims. The neo-Nazi Right has used the influx as a license to express its own Jew-hatred more openly. It has done so in part because the tolerance of Muslim antisemitism has provided an opening for greater expression of antisemitism from other quarters; in part also because the Muslim influx has given rise to wider nativist attitudes, and neo-Nazis have sought to capitalize on this as providing wider receptiveness to their brand of Jew-hatred. It should also be noted that, starting with the rise to power of the Nazis in the 1930s, there has always been some synergy, some mutual support, between the Nazis and neo-Nazis and anti-Jewish, and antizionist, forces in the Arab world, most particularly the Palestinian world. This synergy, discussed in greater detail later, has also been a factor in recent increased expressions of neo-Nazi Jew-hatred.

Antisemitism has for almost two centuries been a staple within the Far Left in Europe, if somewhat muted in the immediate wake of the Holocaust. Those on the European Left who took their cues from Moscow during the Cold War cultivated and promoted an antisemitism in the guise of antizionism. This was so particularly in the wake of the 1967 war and the subsequent dramatic growth in strategic relations between Israel and the United States.

Under the guidance of Moscow, Israel was portrayed as an imperialist outpost of the Americans. Any barrier between antizionism and antisemitism

---

2   Amir Mizroch, "Poll: 90% of ME Views Jews Unfavorably," *Jerusalem Post*, February 9, 2010.

was weak and porous. Jews were often cast as Israel's inevitable supporters, as capitalist anti-leftists and backers of Zionist colonialism. If Jews wanted to be exempted from such condemnation, the onus was on them to prove their worthiness by opposing both Zionism and capitalism. Of course, again as is typical when Jews are under siege, many European Jews were all too ready to accommodate their indicters. This assault on Zionism and Jews has in recent years been perhaps best represented by the Stalinist-style leftist Jeremy Corbyn and his antisemitism-infested British Labor Party.

The influx of Muslims into Europe has been embraced by most of the European Left. The antizionist, and indeed antisemitic, predilections of significant segments of Europe's Left, as well as their open expression of such sentiments, have been reinforced by the desire of the political Left to win and hold the support of the new Muslim citizenry, advancing a Green-Red coalition. If at one time criticism of Israel was moderated in some European settings by a wish to cultivate Jewish support at the polls, those days are long gone as the Muslim electorate far outnumbers the minuscule Jewish communities remaining in virtually all Central and Western European settings. In addition, as with the Far Right, the unabashed public antisemitism promoted by elements of the new Muslim populations has undercut any former prohibitions against such public sentiments and lowered the bar for the expression of similar sentiments by elements of the Far Left.

Similar forces have also been at work in the United States. The immigration of Muslims to America has been on a much smaller scale, in terms of both absolute numbers and proportion of the national population, than such immigration to Central and Western Europe. But elements of the Muslim immigrant population have introduced a new level of antisemitism into the American public arena. In 2017 and early 2018, at least five imams called from their pulpits for attacks on Jews, a theme repeated on numerous other occasions in American mosques and other Muslim venues.[3] Muslim immigrants have been arrested and convicted for plotting the murder of Jews.[4] In the wake

---

3   See, for example, Michael Edison Hayden, "Three U.S. Imams have Called for Death of Jews since Trump's Jerusalem Announcement," *Newsweek*, January 10, 2018. Also, Paul Sperry, "Radical Imams Spewing Anti-Semitism in the U.S. with Impunity," *New York Post*, January 27, 2020.

4   "American Muslim Extremists: A Continuing Threat to Jews," Anti-Defamation League, June 9, 2009; Tina Susman, "Alleged 'Holy War' Plot against Jews, Military Detailed," *Los Angeles Times*, May 22, 2009; Dwight L. Schwab, Jr., "A History of Muslim Murder on American Soil," Newsblaze, April 24, 2013, https://newsblaze.com/thoughts/opinions/a-history-of-muslim-murder-on-american-soil_31734/.

of the October 7, 2023, massacre, the antisemitic fulminations unleashed by American imams have only increased.[5] The first two Muslim women elected to Congress have spewed bigoted anti-Israel diatribes and invoked antisemitic memes, questioning the loyalty of American Jews and claiming Jews have corrupted Congress by buying its support for Israel.[6] Muslim students and faculty on American campuses have been at the forefront not only of promoting the Hamas-linked Boycott, Divestment, and Sanctions (BDS) movement in American colleges and universities but also of initiating assaults, including physical assaults, on Jewish students and faculty.

The Left in America has in recent years favored essentially unfettered illegal immigration into the country through the Mexican border and supported large-scale, largely unvetted immigration from the Middle East. It has done so in part because it has anticipated that would-be immigrants would become reliable Democrat supporters. Much of the mainstream media in America, predominantly Left-leaning, has typically downplayed social and economic difficulties associated with such immigration and has either ignored or downplayed the antisemitism associated with the Muslim immigrant population. In response to the antisemitic comments of the two Muslim women in Congress, the Democrat Congressional delegation could not for a long time bring itself to censure their antisemitism.

On American campuses, largely dominated, like the media, by the Left, except with a greater Marxist bent, faculty members have widely joined in the bigoted demonization of Israel and its American supporters. They have backed the BDS movement and have penalized Jewish students and others who seek to defend Israel. AMCHA, the premiere organization monitoring campus antisemitism, has documented the close correlation between the level of faculty involvement in BDS activism and the targeting of Jewish students on campus.[7]

---

5   See, for example, Ethan Kaufman, "Islamic Preachers in US Escalate Antisemitic Rhetoric amid Gaza War, Campus Protests," *Algemeiner*, May 13, 2024.

6   For example, Philip Klein, "Unrepentant Ilhan Omar Suggests Jews who Criticize Her Anti-Semitic Statements are Doing So because She's Muslim, Revives Dual-Loyalty Smear," *Washington Examiner*, February 28, 2019; Siraj Hachmi, "The Meaning behind Ilhan Omar and Rashida Tlaib's Anti-Semitic Comments," *Washington Examiner*, January 17, 2019; Alexandra Desanctis, "A Congressional Democrat's Latest Anti-Semitic Remark," National Review, May 13, 2019, https://www.nationalreview.com/the-morning-jolt/a-congressional-democrats-latest-anti-semitic-remarks/.

7   See "Academic Agitators: The Role of Anti-Zionist Faculty Activism in Escalating Antisemitism at the University of California after October 7, 2023," AMCHA Initiative, March 2024; "Academic Extremism: How a Faculty Network Fuels Campus Unrest and Antisemitic Violence," AMCHA Initiative, September 2024.

College and university administrators, while typically resisting cooperation in boycotts, have also typically done little to counter campus anti-Israel and anti-Jewish bigotry. While the campuses are the most prominent institutional bastion of antisemitism in today's America, the biased demonization of the Jewish state, and of Jews who support it, has gained ground beyond the campuses and become a staple among many within the so-called "progressive" Left.

Black advocates of radical anti-American agendas have long been open to joining with other minority groups embracing similar agendas, and campuses have been particularly fertile arenas for fostering such alliances. Islamist/ Palestinian BDS activists on campus, particularly Students for Justice in Palestine (SJP), have, in turn, been more than happy to cultivate the support of African American students under the intersectionality umbrella. Faculty members have also been instrumental in promoting the intersectionality gambit, the notion of the common predicament particularly of "people of color" vis-à-vis abuse by dominant Whites. The tack once more serves the Marxist faculty by advancing communal divisions, sowing conflict in a way that simply appealing to class differences could not, and so advancing the Marxist agenda.

Faculties have also worked with Islamist colleagues and students to link the latter's anti-Israel and anti-Jewish activities to the intersectionality bandwagon, with Palestinians now regarded as people of color facing—again, in the meme created and popularized by Soviet propaganda—Western colonialist usurpers. With Black groups on campuses and beyond more than willing to embrace the linkage, the Red-Green alliance has been expanded into a Red-Green-Black antisemitic intersectionality alliance. Faculties, often financed by foreign entities such as Qatar,[8] have also been active in the production and dissemination of curricula for public and private grade schools that convey the intersectionality alliance's anti-Israel and anti-Jewish message. That dissemination has become a widespread project of the Red-Green-Black alliance, infiltrating schools across the nation.

---

8   Adam Kredo, "Qatar Waging Stealth Influence Operations Across U.S. Academic System, Documents Show," *Washington Free Beacon*, May 15, 2020; Jackson Richman, "Qatari Foundation Influences Anti-Israel Propaganda in U.S. Schools," Jewish News Syndicate, October 9, 2018; Sophie Shulman, "Qatar Funds U.S. Universities and Growing Antisemitic Violence in Them," Ynet News, November 11, 2023, https://www.ynetnews.com/business/article/bjldya2qa; "ISGAP Report Examines How Hamas-Harboring Qatar Influences Universities, American Institutions," Institute for the Study of Global Antisemitism and Policy, December 12, 2023.

Hamas, the Palestinian terror group that seized control of Gaza in 2007, two years after Israel's withdrawal from the territory, declares in its charter that its goal is the killing not only of all Israeli Jews but of all Jews worldwide and that this objective is a religious obligation. Its incursion into Israel on October 7, 2023, and the orgy of murder, torture, and mutilation that it unleashed—claiming more than 1,200 lives, with some 240 others taken hostage—was followed by Israel's invasion of Gaza with the intent of uprooting Hamas and destroying its military. Almost immediately in the wake of October 7, demonstrations of support for the Islamist organization along with a storm of antisemitic words and deeds filled American campuses and the streets of major American cities. The outpouring of anti-Jewish vitriol gave dramatic illustration of how far the American version of the Red-Green-Black alliance had propelled Jew-hatred within significant segments of the nation.

But while there were widespread expressions of astonishment and disbelief at the level of antisemitism displayed in marches and other actions across America, no one who had been paying attention was surprised. The response, for example, to the May 2021 Israel-Gaza war was no less bigoted and ugly. The 2021 war was the fourth triggered in thirteen years by Hamas rocket and missile attacks on Israel. The reaction from much of the Red-Green-Black alliance—then as in October 2023—was support for Hamas, or silence with regard to its genocidal agenda and war-crime actions, along with demonization of Israel and its American supporters and an unbridled outpouring of antisemitic diatribes and actions, with assaults on Jews and Jewish institutions. The attacks swept over the nation's campuses and beyond, and the reprise of those attacks in their antizionist guise filled much of the left-leaning mainstream media and could be heard even in the halls of Congress.

Leaders of the Black Lives Matter organization condemned Israel in the context of the fighting and declared the organization's "solidarity with Palestine."[9] For some years BLM leaders have embraced the Hamas-linked Boycott, Divestment, and Sanctions movement against Israel[10] and at times have called for Israel's annihilation.[11] In recent years, Black Lives Matter "demonstrators"

---

9   Lee Brown, "Black Lives Matter Comes Out in Solidarity with Palestinians," *New York Post*, May 19, 2021.

10 Alexa George, "Black Lives Matter Endorses BDS, Says Israel Perpetuates 'Genocide,'" Arab America, August 5, 2016, https://www.arabamerica.com/black-lives-matter-endorses-bds-says-israel-perpetuates-genocide/.

11 For example, Samuel Chamberlain, "BLM Co-Founder Called in 2015 to 'End the Imperialist Project' of Israel," *New York Post*, May 30, 2021.

have vandalized synagogues and Jewish businesses in Los Angeles and elsewhere.[12] They have done all this while playing up the intersectionality connection between African-Americans and Palestinians. The assertion by BLM leaders of their immersion in and embrace of Marxist/Communist ideology represents another stream of Jew-hatred shaping the organization's actions. BLM support for the genocidally antisemitic Hamas in the recent war is thus of a piece with the organization's longstanding and much-reiterated positions.

A number of African American members of Congress echoed BLM's intersectionality-infused pro-Hamas stance. Congresswoman Ayanna Pressley opined: "Palestinians are being told the same thing as black folks in America—there is no acceptable form of resistance."[13] The implication seemed to be that Hamas's missiles, and its underlying agenda, should be seen as "acceptable forms of resistance." Congresswoman Cori Bush likewise drew an analogy between Blacks in America and the Palestinians and appeared to justify Hamas's missile barrages as part of "the fight for Palestinian liberation," which she saw as "interconnected" with the struggles of African Americans.[14] Congressman Jamaal Bowman also took up this supposed interconnection: "Enough of Black and brown bodies being brutalized and murdered," he expounded, echoing Hamas's propaganda and lies.[15]

Of course, various other members of Congress likewise blamed Israel for the 2021 hostilities and either explicitly or implicitly sided with Hamas. Ilhan Omar and Rashida Tlaib, Muslim Congresswomen with histories of trafficking in antisemitic tropes, predictably came out with attacks on Israel. Omar essentially called for Israel's destruction. Tlaib characterized the Palestinians as passive victims of Israeli aggression. Neither mentioned Hamas's missile onslaught.[16] Both women have invoked the intersectionality link with African Americans to buttress their anti-Israel and anti-Jewish agendas.

---

12 See, for example, Joshua Washington, "Black Lives Matter's Jewish Problem—In Their Own Words," *Times of Israel*, August 7, 2020.

13 "Rep. Pressley Delivers Floor Speech on Israeli State Violence and Human Rights Abuse in Palestine," Congresswoman Ayanna Pressley, May 13, 2021, https://pressley.house.gov/2021/05/13/rep-pressley-delivers-floor-speech-israeli-state-violence-and-human-rights/.

14 Ayara Pommels, "Rep. Cori Bush: "The Fight for Black Lives and Palestinian Liberation are Interconnected," Hub News, May 17, 2021, https://thehub.news/rep-cori-bush-the-fight-for-black-lives-and-palestinian-liberation-are-interconnected/.

15 Jamaal Bowman, "Enough of Black and brown bodies being brutalized and murdered," Twitter, May 11, 2021, https://x.com/JamaalBowmanNY/status/1392056693433962498.

16 See, for example, "Congress Members Slam US Support for Israel," Aljazeera, May 14, 2021.

Representing the anti-Israel agenda of the Red-Green-Black alliance's progressive/Far Left contingent, a number of whose Congressional adherents signed an anti-Israel letter during the war, Congresswoman Ocasio-Cortes suggested that Israel's response to the Hamas missile barrages was somehow an attack on Palestinians' "right to survive" and that Hamas's missiles were defending that right.[17]

Twenty-five members of Congress signed the anti-Israel letter, initiated by Representatives Marie Newman and Mark Pocan, again condemning Israel with absurd charges and without referencing Hamas's initiation of the war or intentional targeting of civilians.[18] Of the twenty-five signers, seventeen had also sent letters of congratulations and support in November 2019 to the Council on American-Islamic Relations (CAIR) on the occasion of its gala celebration. (Ilhan Omar was a featured speaker at the event.) CAIR had earlier been named by the FBI as an unindicted co-conspirator in the Holy Land Foundation trial for providing backchannel financial support to Hamas and being part of a group set up by the Muslim Brotherhood for that purpose.[19]

On the nation's campuses, beyond the many faculty resolutions condemning Israel and siding with Hamas, student groups reflecting the intersectional Red-Green-Black alliance likewise passed anti-Israel, in effect pro-Hamas, resolutions and demonstrated in support of that agenda.

On the streets of cities across the nation, Jews and Jewish institutions were attacked by Palestinian/Islamist assailants often joined by intersectionality allies.

The Red-Green-Black Alliance and White Supremacists/Neo-Nazis

The tsunami of antisemitic acts that accompanied the 2021 war also underscored another element of the Red-Green-Black alliance's intersectional

---

17 Akshita Jain, "Do Palestinians have a Right to Survive? AOC Makes Impassioned Speech against Biden Policy on Israel Crisis," *Independent*, May 14, 2021.

18 See, for example, Jordan Boyd, "Leftist Legislators Launch Anti-Israel Tirades on Twitter as Hamas Bombs Jewish Cities," *Federalist*, May 13, 2021.

19 See, for example, Robert Spencer, "More than 120 Members of Congress Issue Letters of Support to Hamas-Linked CAIR," Jihad Watch, January 19, 2020, https://jihadwatch. org/2020/01/more-than-120-members-of-congress-issue-letters-of-support-to-hamas-linked-cair.

Jew-hatred: its links to neo-Nazi and white supremacist Jew-hatred. Ostensibly, the antisemitism of African-American groups such as the Black Lives Matter organization and its Congressional auxiliary is grounded in Jews being white and beneficiaries of white privilege; and the antisemitism of Islamist/Palestinian allies of Black Jew-haters and Jew baiters is due to Israeli colonialism and, again, a response to white imperialism; and both groups' leftist/Marxist allies, on and off campus, either tacitly or explicitly endorse these rationales for attacks on the Jews. But the concerns about white privilege and white imperialism and white supremacism somehow have not prevented the intersectionality alliance from finding common ground with neo-Nazis and white supremacists.

The Right in America has opposed the large-scale illegal immigration across the southern border, and the white supremacist Right, like the neo-Nazi Right in Europe, has sought to build on broader discontent with this immigration to expand its own numbers. It has also, as in Europe, built on the tolerance of public expressions of Muslim antisemitism, the lowered bar to public spewing of antisemitism, as license for its own voicing of antisemitic venom. In some ways, the American racist Right has even surpassed the neo-Nazi European Right in its rhetoric. It has proclaimed, as a central tenet of its propaganda, that illegal immigration is actually a Jewish plot to replace the "white race" in America. The notion of a "great replacement" being promoted by globalist elites is popular among right-wing groups in Europe, but it seems among white supremacists in America that mass immigration has been more emphatically cast as a Jewish plot.

The increasing attacks on Jews by intersectional allies, including the attacks around the 2021 war, and the frequent association on social media of intersectional allies' anti-Israel and anti-Jewish memes with praise of Hitler, have led a number of commentators to look at the connections between those allies and Far Right antisemites.

With regard to Islamists and Palestinian leaders, there is not far to look. Islamism, or Islamic supremacist ideology wedded to Jihad, has almost invariably had a prominent following within the faith and has tended to come to the fore in the context of difficulties in the Muslim world. Thus, European colonial inroads into that world in the nineteenth and early twentieth centuries and the embrace of Western culture by many in, for example, the Muslim Middle East, led to an Islamist reaction. According to that reaction, the end of Muslim expansion and the success of European political and cultural encroachment were made possible by Muslims falling away from rigorous adherence to their faith, and the remedy lay in rededication to militant Islam and Jihad.

This comprehension of Muslim religious duty, most notably represented by the Muslim Brotherhood, spread rapidly in the Arab world in the early twentieth century and subsequently went well beyond that world. The Brotherhood, the major source of contemporary Islamism, virtually from its inception viewed European fascism, including Nazism, as a model for building an anti-Western movement and exposing and challenging the perceived corruption, decadence, and vulnerability of the Western democracies. The Nazis' targeting of the Jews converged with the Islamist animus against both Christians and Jews but particularly against the latter. Jews were perceived as the weakest of peoples, and their achievements within Western societies were therefore seen as further evidence of the West's decadence and as a further insult to Muslims who had been bested and overtaken in political and military power by those societies. (Just as, for example, the tolerance of Jews in then cosmopolitan Egypt was viewed by the Muslim Brotherhood as a sign of the decadence of Egyptian society and the necessity of an Islamist revolution.) Jews were also seen, as in fascist Europe, as a vulnerable and despised target useful for advancing a political movement. As a phrase popularized by Islamists—to capture a strategic sequencing of targets—puts it: First Saturday's people, then Sunday's people; or, first Jerusalem, then Rome.

Among Palestinians, Haj Amin al-Husseini, the grand mufti of Jerusalem and premier Palestinian leader who in 1929 and again in 1936–1939 orchestrated deadly attacks on Jews, supported Nazi operations in the Middle East. He subsequently went to Berlin, where he remained through much of the war as Hitler's guest—perhaps the original intersectionality—recruiting southern European Muslims for the SS and broadcasting calls to the Arab world to support the Nazis and kill Jews. He also planned with Nazi officials arrangements for the extermination of the Jews of the Palestine Mandate after what was anticipated to be either Nazi military penetration of the Middle East via the Caucasus or Rommel's Afrika Korps's conquest of Egypt and advancement eastward.[20] Al-Husseini remains a revered and inspiring figure for Palestinian leaders and their followers.

As does Hitler; and not only among Palestinians. He's admired in the wider Muslim world, particularly where the Muslim Brotherhood and its offshoots, such as Hamas, have political and cultural influence and a following.

---

20 See, for example, Klaus-Michael Mallmann and Martin Cuppers, *Nazi Palestine: The Plans for the Extermination of the Jews of Palestine* (New York: Enigma, 2013); Edy Cohen, "The Grand Mufti's Nazi Connection," *Jerusalem Post*, April 7, 2014.

Statements from Palestinians and others in the Muslim world to the effect that Hitler was right, or that he didn't kill enough Jews, or that the world needs a Hitler now—views that many would imagine are limited to neo-Nazis and white supremacists—are common in that world. So, too, is the publication and wide dissemination of *Mein Kampf*. They reflect what has long been popular sentiment.

Matthias Kuntzel, in *Jihad and Jew-Hatred*, traces the Nazis' dealings with the Muslim Brotherhood and other Islamists before and during World War II and the Nazis' role in amplifying and shaping Muslim antisemitism since the war. Kuntzel refers in the book to

> the circulation with express PA [Palestinian Authority] approval of Hitler's programmatic work *Mein Kampf*, which reached number six on the Palestinian Territory's bestseller list in 1999. The translator of the Arabic edition refers in his introduction to his author's continued relevance: "Adolf Hitler does not belong to the German people alone, he is one of the few great men who almost stopped the motion of history, altered its course . . . National Socialism did not die with the death of its herald. Rather, its seeds multiplied under each star."[21]

It should come as no surprise then that Islamists and Palestinians in the West, including the United States, should express similar sentiments on social media in Europe and America. The use of Nazi caricatures of Jews and other elements of Nazi propaganda are likewise widespread and popular in the Palestinian and wider Muslim world and also find their way onto Western social media from Islamist and Palestinian sources.

Mohammed Al-Azdee, an Iraqi-born scholar who had served as associate professor of communication theory at Bridgeport University, has documented the extensive use of weekly sermons by imams in American mosques to promote Jew-hatred and incite anti-Jewish violence. His research was reviewed in an article by Ben Cohen,[22] who notes that, according to Al-Azdee,

---

21 Matthias Kuntzel, *Jihad and Jew-Hatred* (Candor, NY: Telos Press, 2009), 117. Kuntzel cites "Hitler's Mein Kampf in East Jerusalem and PA Territories," Middle East Media Research Institute (MEMRI), Special Dispatch no. 48, October 1, 1999.

22 Ben Cohen, "Entrenched Antisemitism among Imams Serving US Moslem Communities Need to Be Challenged, Scholar Tells Major Conference," *Algemeiner*, July 20, 2021.

Key [to the anti-Jewish content of the sermons] is the linkage between the nature of antisemitism among Islamists and that of the Nazi regime in Germany. . . . Bridging these two worlds, Al-Azdee points out, were a series of theologians and political leaders, such as Sayyid Qutb, the chief ideologue of the Muslim Brotherhood in Egypt in the middle of the last century; Hajj Amin al-Husseini . . . and the late Al Qaeda chieftain Osama bin Laden, whose 2002 letter to the American people informed them that they could not be considered "innocent of all the crimes committed by the Americans and Jews against us . . ."

"There are links to major antisemitic traditions," Al-Azdee said. "Nazi propaganda shaped Arab antisemitism, and in my data analysis you can see the pattern of alignment between Nazi and Muslim antisemitism. The khutbahs [sermons] are about Jews, but Jews represented as 'Der ewige Jude'—'The Eternal Jew,' the German title of a 1940 propaganda film backed by Hitler's Minister of Propaganda, Josef Goebbels, which purported to unveil a global Jewish conspiracy against Germany."

The range of antisemitic themes pushed by the imams examined by Al-Azdee also conformed to the various Nazi obsessions about Jews, from possessing unaccountable economic power to corrupting the morals of society. As Sayyid Qutb venomously put it, "from such creatures who kill and massacre and defame prophets, one can only expect the spilling of human blood and of dirty means that will further their machinations and evil."

According to Al-Azdee, for Qutb and other Islamist ideologues, antisemitism was an "integral component of the Islamic state," much as it was in Germany under National Socialism. That view is buttressed by antisemitic quotes from the Qu'ran as well as from the hadiths, or sayings, of the Prophet Muhammad, describing Jews as the descendants of "apes and pigs," urging their execution on the "Day of Judgement," and labeling them as "filth"—a term that in the Muslim world, Al-Azdee said, refers explicitly to human excrement.

The Islamist theme of contemptible Jewish weakness, with any Jewish success in competition with, or even in comparison to, Muslims therefore being a particular insult to Islam, would seem inconsistent with Islamist promotion of the Nazi-inspired theme of Jewish satanic power that represents an existential threat to Islam. But they are simply two jointly exploited versions of anti-Jewish defamation. They are similar to the Islamists/Palestinians at once denying the Holocaust, accusing the Jews of being mass murderers like the Nazis, and insisting that Hitler was a hero who should have killed more Jews and should be emulated.

Pro-Nazi rhetoric is also a major element of the campus activism of Arab and other Muslim students and faculty, who are largely aligned with the rejectionist Muslim Brotherhood or the Iran regime rather than with the Arab states that are pursuing rapprochement with Israel. Many of the activists, like their heroes in Hamas, Hezbollah and similar groups, openly advocate the genocide of the Jews on social media and declare their admiration for Hitler and the Nazis.[23]

Among African Americans, there have also long been pro-Nazi and pro-Hitler contingents. This has particularly been so within Black radical movements. As Daniel Greenfield relates, in an article entitled "Hitler's Multicultural Supporters,"[24] Malcolm X "welcomed the leader of the American Nazi Party . . . to a Nation of Islam event." Malcolm X also met with leaders of the KKK, and he met as well with and spoke positively of Haj Amin al-Husseini. The Nation of Islam's Louis Farrakhan, amid his Jew-baiting rants, has declared that "Hitler was a very great man," and, of course, he has parroted Nazi characterizations of Jews as subhuman. The virulent antisemite Stokeley Carmichael/Kwame Ture asserted, "We must take a lesson from Hitler"; and "I've never admired a white man, but the greatest of them, to my mind, was Hitler." At a time when Black radicalism and separatism is again in vogue, cheered on by academia and its promotion of separate Black living quarters, social spaces, even graduation ceremonies, it is not surprising that pro-Nazi and white supremacist anti-Jewish tropes would be more prominently incorporated into some arenas of Black political discourse. The citation at the opening of the chapter, noting former Black congresswoman

---

23   See, for example, Sara Dogan, "Texas SJP and MSA Activists Revealed as Neo-Nazis in Poster Campaign: Students Advocate Violence against Jews, Praise Adolf Hitler," *Frontpage*, March 23, 2018.
24   Daniel Greenfield, "Hitler's Multicultural Supporters," *Frontpage*, June 4, 2021.

Cynthia McKinney's enthusiastically publicizing a livestream event of ex-KKK grand wizard David Duke and a Black nationalist talking about joining forces to attack the "common enemy," the Jews, is just one recent iteration of this phenomenon.

At the same time, white supremacists and neo-Nazis have taken up Black radical/supremacist and Islamist/Palestinian tropes. What we have is white supremacists and Black radicals as well as Islamist/Palestinian supremacists sharing and trafficking in each other's antisemitic fabrications and calumnies. Add in the Jew-hatred emanating from progressive and neo-Marxist circles and one captures something of the breadth, and depth, of the antisemitic onslaught; an onslaught in the face of which the Jewish communal response has been much too weak.

Chapter Three

American Jewish Communal Failure

"What is Critical Race Theory and Why is It in the News So Much"
An Anti-Defamation League publication (November 15, 2021) supporting Critical Race
Theory (CRT) and Diversity, Equity, and Inclusion (DEI) and ignoring the recurrent presence
of attacks on Jews and Israel in CRT and DEI-related programs, including in grade schools.

American Jewish organizations, including the Anti-Defamation League, have generally been much more sensitive and responsive to antisemitism coming from the Right in America, whether in traditional antisemitic forms or in the form of bigoted attacks on the Jewish state, than to similar sentiments emanating from other sources. This pattern has continued in the current climate of increased antisemitism. It is true that the murders of Jews in Pittsburgh and Poway were perpetrated by espousers of white supremacist sentiments, while other white supremacists have been apprehended planning to murder Jews. Some Jews and Jewish groups have sought to justify the focus on rightist antisemitism by citing this reality. But people motivated by different political sentiments have also physically attacked Jews, have called for their murder and planned their murder, and at times have actually carried out murderous assaults, as in Jersey City, Monsey and, of course, Washington, D.C. Numerous arrests and prosecutions for such attacks and plans have involved denizens of the Red-Green-Black alliance.

The response of mainstream Jewish organizations to antisemitism emanating from left-wing, African American and Muslim sources has been so weak as to often be virtually non-existent. Indeed, it has not been uncommon for these organizations and their leaders to defend the progressive Left as well as hostile Muslim groups and African-American groups such as Black Lives Matter against criticism from Jews who seek to challenge the hatred coming from those sources. This is true even as leftist, Islamist, and Black radical antisemitism has penetrated much more into the American mainstream than has Far Right antisemitism.

The Anti-Defamation League was the most prominent signer of a full-page Jewish ad in the *New York Times* in August 2020, backing BLM.[1] Its national director and CEO, Jonathan Greenblatt, tweeted his pride in an earlier iteration of the pro-BLM statement. The ADL, in contorted defenses of BLM, has claimed that the group is loosely organized, and that anti-Jewish acts and statements are the work of peripheral figures.[2] But, in fact, as already noted, figures among the founders and current leaders of BLM have both voiced antisemitic vitriol and played a role in anti-Jewish acts. While offering little in the way of calling out politicians on the Left given to antisemitism, including Ilhan Omar, Greenblatt was quick to praise Omar for her partial distancing herself from one of her numerous anti-Jewish statements.[3]

Even in the wake of the October 7, 2023, massacre in Israel and the extensive pro-Hamas response in America—a response overwhelmingly emanating from bastions of the Left, most notably academia, and from Islamist and Black radical sources—the initial ADL reaction was to focus on the antisemitism of the Far Right. On October 10, it published a report entitled "White Supremacist Leaders Applaud Hamas Violence Against Israelis," documenting the celebratory spewings in online posts by several neo-Nazi and white supremacist leaders and groups. The ADL offered no comparable reports on Islamists and progressives and Black radicals who, at the same time and in much greater number, were celebrating Hamas and cursing Israel and Jews. On the contrary, it continued, for example, to defend its long support

1   "600-Plus Jewish Groups Sign Full-Page Ad Supporting Black Lives Matter," Jewish News Syndicate, August 28, 2020.
2   See, for example, ADL statements cited in Tom Kertscher, "Ask PolitiFact: Is Black Lives Matter anti-Semitic?," PolitiFact, August 24, 2020, https://www.politifact.com/article/2020/aug/24/ask-politifact-black-lives-matter-anti-semitic/.
3   See, for example, Hagay Hacohen, "ADL Chief Too Quick to Forgive Rep. Omar for Antisemitic Comment: ZOA," Jerusalem Post, January 29, 2019.

for Black Lives Matter despite the full-throated defamation of Israel and backing of Hamas proffered by major chapters of the organization in the wake of the October 7 slaughter.

On October 31, 2023, the *Wall Street Journal* published an op-ed by Jason Riley entitled "Black Lives Matter and the World's Oldest Hatred." Riley documents the long history of anti-Israel invective, including accusations of genocide, coming from major figures in the organization. He writes,

> What's shocking isn't the rhetoric of BLM leaders in the aftermath of Oct. 7 but that so many people who ought to have known better got played. In 2020, an open letter that endorsed the BLM movement appeared as a full-page ad in the New York Times. It was signed by more than 600 Jewish organizations, including the Anti-Defamation League, which exists to fight anti-Semitism. If accusing Israel of genocide isn't defamation of Jewish people, I don't know what is. Yet Jonathan Greenblatt, the executive director of the Anti-Defamation League, is a prominent defender of BLM.

Riley then cites Greenblatt on BLM:

> "There are those who are attempting to smear this movement as inherently anti-Semitic," Mr. Greenblatt wrote in a September 2020 Medium post. "It is not." He added that while "some individuals and organizations associated with the Black Lives Matter movement have engaged in antisemitic rhetoric," it "would be foolish to cede the conversation to the most intemperate voices."

Greenblatt responded to Riley's op-ed with a November 5 letter to the editor in which he again disingenuously suggests that only certain chapters of BLM engage in antisemitic and anti-Israel vitriol. He then seeks to justify his embrace of BLM by noting the historic importance of the Black-Jewish alliance, seeming to aver, delusionally, that BLM is part of such an alliance.

Certainly, the ADL has not been alone among Jewish groups in giving a pass to many of those purveying antisemitism in America. The list of organizations doing so—both mainstream bodies and those more marginal groups who make common cause with non-Jewish circles that advocate Israel's destruction and defame the American Jewish community—is long indeed. The Jewish pro-BLM ad in *The New York Times* had, as Riley noted, more than 600 institutional signers along with the ADL.[4]

Again, American academia is the nation's most significant institutional generator of antisemitism, fomenting broad faculty and student antagonism towards Israel and towards Jews on campus. As always in Jewish history (as similarly in the history of other minorities) the more intense the onslaught the more inevitable is the phenomenon of elements of the Jewish community joining the attackers. Thus, one has Jewish Voice for Peace joining the BDS mobs, calling for the dissolution of Israel, allying itself with a genocidal Hamas, and latterly carrying its anti-Israel campaign beyond the campuses. A similar agenda has animated the group IfNotNow. Another group of the same ilk is the Soros-funded Bend the Arc, perhaps most known for its championing of antisemites such as Linda Sarsour who seek to exclude Jews from feminist and other "progressive" events.

The appearance under siege conditions of such anti-Jewish Jewish groups is, as already suggested, virtually inevitable; it has always been thus. What is less inevitable and more troubling is the failure of mainstream Jewish groups to address the antisemitism of the campuses or of the campus antisemites' fellow-travelers among Jews. The main establishment Jewish organization on American campuses is Hillel, with a presence at more than 500 colleges and universities. Some Hillel chapters seek forcefully to pursue equitable treatment for Jews and for Israel on campus. But many do not, preferring instead to equivocate or be silent in the face of the targeting of Jews and of Israel, or even to seek to accommodate anti-Israel sentiment in their programming. They will also counsel Jewish students against organizing on their own against anti-Jewish depredations, and will seek to undermine such efforts. The negative impact on Jewish students who might otherwise relish strongly opposing anti-Israel activity is one more data point in the calculus of Jewish leadership dereliction. In addition, many Hillel chapters choose to embrace those Jewish voices hostile to Israel, in the service of what they argue to be a necessary

---

4   For more on the signers of the ad, see, for example, "ZOA Criticizes ADL, Reform/ Conservative Movements, JCRCs, HIAS, Etc., Signing Ad Supporting Israel- and Jew-Hating Black Lives Matter Organization, Co-Signed with Israel-Haters," Zionist Organization of America, September 13, 2020; Jonathan Tobin, "What are Jews who Embrace the Black Lives Matter Movement Endorsing?" Israel National News, September 1, 2020.

"big tent," finding room for all "Jewish" opinion. Is it really reasonable to accommodate those Jews who advocate the destruction of the Jewish state?

Beyond the failure of key mainstream Jewish communal organizations to address effectively the rising antisemitism in the nation and counter the institutions that are fostering it and trafficking in it, those organizations are failing to address other related threats to American Jews. Basic American "liberal" principles (that is, "liberal" in the traditional sense), which have figured prominently in making the Jewish experience in America so much more benign than elsewhere, have in recent years come under attack, and primarily from the Left. What is more fundamental to American Jewish well-being than the First Amendment and freedom of speech? Equally fundamental to that well-being is the principle embodied in Martin Luther King's vision of a more fully realized adherence to judging people by the content of their character rather than the color of their skin or, by extension, their ethnicity or religion or gender or some other element of group identity. Yet both principles are under incessant attack in the leftist-dominated academy, where a supposed "right" to protection from distressing ideas trumps freedom of speech and where group identity trumps individual identity. And these illiberal principles are spreading out from our colleges and universities to other bastions of the Left. Censorship of unapproved ideas is now advocated and practiced by the overwhelmingly leftist mainstream media and social media, and it is aggressively promoted and advanced by the progressive wing of the Democrat Party. And Jews have, in fact, been particularly hurt by these developments. Yet there has been no substantive Jewish organizational response.

The widespread eruption of anti-Israel and anti-Jewish rhetoric on US campuses in the wake of the October 7, 2023, massacre in Israel was accompanied by many college and university administrators hypocritically invoking first amendment rights—more honored in their breach than in their enforcement in today's academia—to justify their tolerating this hatefest. Some leaders of mainstream Jewish organizations did eventually note the hypocrisy and the reality that similar hateful language towards virtually any other minority group would not be accorded such tolerance. But, overall, the Jewish organizational response remained woefully inadequate.

In the months following the Hamas invasion and slaughter and the campus reaction, the Anti-Defamation League put together and posted a "Campus Anti-Semitism Report Card," which it characterized as "a tool for students, parents, alumni, college faculty, guidance counselors, admissions consultants and other stakeholders. Our goal is to serve students and their families looking for information about the current state of antisemitism on campus and how particular universities and colleges are responding." The report card, acknowledged to be a work in progress, graded several dozen colleges and universities and assigned the great majority grades of C or below. The ADL also got involved in taking legal action against some educational institutions.

At the same time, the ADL's online "Hate Symbols Database" offered 214 examples of symbols and the hate groups using them, all neo-Nazi, white racist, and related groups. There are zero examples of antisemitic Islamist groups and their symbols then proliferating on campuses. As one observer noted in a televised report: "When the protests broke out at Columbia University and spread to campuses across the country, it was only natural for terrorist organizations to express their support. The flags, logos, signs, posters, patches, headbands and other paraphernalia of Hamas, Hezbollah and the [Popular] Front for the Liberation of Palestine (PFLP), are visible and have often gone viral on social media."[5] Likewise on prominent display on campuses but omitted from the ADL inventory of hate symbols were those exhibited by Far Left groups, such as stars of David crossed out or equated to swastikas. In a similar vein, the ADL's "Glossary of Extremism and Hate" is overwhelmingly focused on terminology associated with white racist and neo-Nazi groups, although a small number of terms and labels related to Islamist and other hate groups are included.

Also noteworthy is that the ADL website, under "Mission and History," lists accomplishments by decade starting with the 1910s. Among those cited for the 1950s is, "ADL publishes the 1952 exposé, *The Troublemakers*, documenting how Arab propaganda in the U.S. explicitly sought to foment anti-Israel and anti-Jewish sentiments." For the 1970s it notes, among other entries,

> The Yom Kippur War in 1973 intensifies ADL's campaign to counter anti-Israel propaganda. The agency exposes and takes the lead in combating the Arab boycott of companies that do business with Israel, leading to the passage of the 1977 and 1978 laws that prohibit American companies from participating in the blacklist.
>
> Using all media at its disposal, ADL exposes Palestinian Liberation Organization and Arab links to terrorism and

5   Steven Stalinsky, "College Protests Reveal Alarming Terrorist Support. And Jihadists Cheer Them On," Fox News, May 16, 2024.

highlights the hypocrisy of a United Nations General Assembly resolution equating Zionism with racism.

The counteraction leads to the publication of ADL's *The New Anti-Semitism*, a book documenting worldwide insensitivity and indifference to a campaign that denies Israel its legitimacy as the Jewish national homeland.

The entries for the 2020s include: "In May 2021, amid an escalation of conflict between Hamas militants and Israel, ADL tracks and monitors a rise in antisemitic incidents in the U.S. and around the world, providing resources to report these incidents and statements supporting a peaceful resolution to the hostilities." And: "In response to the horrific October 7, 2023, Hamas attack on Israel and subsequent global surge in antisemitism, ADL stands in solidarity with Israel—and as a leading voice against antisemitism and hate." While there are several entries on hatred more generally and what the ADL construes as other hate-related developments, and on a few Far Right domestic groups associated with them, there is no reference to the Islamist, Far Left, and Black radical groups responsible for so much of the domestic upsurge of antisemitism. There is also no equivalent to the 1950s entry on foreign entities promoting Israel-hatred and Jew-hatred in America, although the problem has become much worse than it was then.

An ADL solicitation letter, sent out as the 2024 Jewish High Holidays and the anniversary of the October 7 massacre approached, opened with the story of a family terrorized by Far Right bigots. No other characterization of hatred's perpetrators was cited in the appeal. The same was true of another solicitation letter sent out at the end of the calendar year.

Why is the response to palpable threats from the progressive/Marxist Left, from Black radicals, from Palestinian/Islamist supremacists, and from their institutional allies on the campuses, in the media, among cultural elites, and in the Democrat Party, so weak? While the predilection of a substantial part of the community to strive to ingratiate itself with its abusers is the key factor, the supine reaction to the current anti-Jewish assaults requires more detailed examination of how that predilection is now manifesting itself.

In recent centuries, in the context of the emergence of modern nation states, the issue of extending civic rights to Jews was broached in various Central European polities. Those against doing so would raise numerous bigoted objections. For example, they argued that the Jews were largely engaged in commerce, which was a degenerate enterprise and rendered them unfit for civic rights. And they spoke a degenerate language, Yiddish, which also rendered them unfit. And, it was asserted, they were only interested in their coreligionists rather than others outside their community, and this, too, rendered them unfit. As discussed in the next chapter, every objection, however bigoted, had its Jewish endorsers, who urged reform to remove the taint and win over the haters.

Obviously, not everyone in the community was given to embracing the indictments of the haters. Many pursued the more constructive path of cultivating ties with whatever elements in the broader society were more receptive to extending civic rights to Jews. (This was not an either/or choice. Some Jews tried to propitiate the haters through self-reform and also to seek out less hostile groups in the broader society.) In general, although it did not always fall out this way, those in Prussia and other pre-unification German states of Central Europe who were more receptive to the cause of Jewish civic rights tended to fall on the more liberal side of the contemporary political spectrum, while those less receptive tended to be associated with more conservative circles.

But even in cultivating this course of seeking out, and aligning with, seemingly sympathetic elements in the wider society, those in the Jewish community, and within the community leadership, who did so very often behaved in a manner that still reflected self-delusions characteristic of chronically besieged populations. For one, as will be illustrated in the next chapter, in their desperation for allies to help counter their vulnerability, they not uncommonly deluded themselves into categorical thinking about such political alliances. They were inclined to believe that, if properly cultivated, these unions would represent transcendent connections that would inevitably endure. Other, less marginal, groups in the society would recognize that political alliances could shift and that today's shared agenda may not last. But the Jews' eagerness for protection from vulnerability via alliances often led a large part of the community to close its eyes to this reality and let its wishful thinking distort its vision.

Particularly after the failure of the 1848 revolutions, Jews from the German states of Central Europe emigrated in significant numbers to America and brought their political predilections with them. The same is true of the Eastern European Jewish immigrants, primarily from pogrom-wracked czarist Russia, at the end of the century. As discussed in the next chapter, their political predilections differed somewhat from those of the German Jewish immigrants, but they were marked by similar self-defeating patterns. And, as addressed in Chapter Five, the maladaptive patterns of both groups' predilections have continued in the United States. Delusional categorical thinking about allies and enemies, the wishful belief that the community can immerse itself in an immutable political alliance which will assure its well-being, has persisted. So too has the related delusion that an agenda of embracing the perceived allies of the Jewish community, even if that commitment is not reciprocated, will serve to advance the Jews' security by assuaging accusations of parochialism and narrow self-interest. These twin driving forces continue to shape the Jews' often dangerously self-defeating political choices. A major element of this problematic thinking was noted by the sociologists Seymour Martin Lipset and Earl Raab in 1995 when they pointed out that American Jews have persistently believed antisemitism to be more rife among American conservatives than among liberals, even though actual surveys of American opinion regarding Jews have not supported this assumption.[6]

In our times, a large part of the Jewish community and an even greater percentage of its leadership have long failed to address adequately or indeed acknowledge antisemitism coming from sources other than white supremacist and neo-Nazi groups, even as other sources of Jew-hatred, largely leftist ones, have penetrated much more into the wider society. They have failed to call out and challenge the antisemitism of the progressive Left, which is now even on display in the halls of Congress. Even as the assault on Jews by Black radical groups, by Islamist/Palestinian groups, and by the Far Left in the universities and elsewhere becomes more commonplace and more rabid, the response of much of the Jewish leadership and many of its followers— including in the wake of October 7, 2023—has evolved at most from virtual silence to falling still woefully short of what is needed.

And that muted response does not simply mean that the purveyors of antisemitism can proceed essentially unchallenged. It actually acts as an accelerant to antisemitism, contributing to its increase, its greater penetration into American society, and its normalization. Consider the Democrat Party's tolerance of antisemitic spewings by the likes of Ilhan Omar and Rashida Tlaib, or the party's according a prominent role to notorious antisemites at the 2020 Democrat convention,[7] or, as discussed later, all that has followed

6   Seymour Martin Lipset and Earl Raab, *Jews and the New American Scene* (Cambridge, MA: Harvard University Press, 1995), 152.

7   See, for example, press release, "ZOA Horrified: Antisemites/Israel-Haters Linda Sarsour, Tamika Mallory, Imam Hussain, AOC, Others Speak at Democratic Nat'l Convention," Zionist Organization of America, August 21, 2020, https://zoa.

since then in a similar vein. If there is no Jewish pushback, no price paid by the party for indulging antisemites, and only support for that indulgence from the other side—from Far Left progressives, Black radicals, and Islamists/Palestinians—what incentive does the party have to rein it in?

Even more destructive is, of course, the support given to non-Far Right antisemites by mainstream Jewish organizations, most notably the ADL. Beyond those examples already cited, and much more consequential, is—as revealed in an exposé in September 2022[8]—the ADL's distribution of "educational" materials supposedly aimed at fighting bias and hatred but actually supporting leftist cant that entails antisemitic tropes and legitimizing groups which promote Jew-hatred. The ADL claimed in 2021 that its "anti-bias" programs reached over 46,000 educators and nearly five million K-12 students. The exposé showed that those programs included promotion of critical race theory, which not only falsely stigmatizes America as systemically racist and addicted to white privilege but also pushes the characterization of Jews as exploiters of white privilege who can have no legitimate claim to being victims of bias. The ADL materials also lent support to the Women's March despite its leaders pushing Jew-hatred. In addition, the materials backed the intersectionality crusade, ignoring its chronic attacks on Israel and on American Jews, and continued the ADL's championing of Black Lives Matter while remaining silent on the movement's antizionism and antisemitism. At a time when trafficking in antisemitism by groups not associated with the extreme Right had reached unprecedented levels in the United States, what was once the premiere American Jewish organization opposing antisemitism had instead, in an unconscionable betrayal of the American Jewish community, become largely a supporter and enabler of those groups. As noted, since the October 7, 2023, massacre ADL has taken some steps to address the anti-Jewish onslaught from sources other than the Far Right, particularly from academia.

---

org/2020/08/10441087-zoa-horrified-antisemites-israel-haters-linda-sarsour-tami-ka-mallory-imam-hussain-aoc-others-speak-at-democratic-natl-convention/.

8   See, for example, Jonathan Tobin's interview of William Jacobson, "ADL is 'mired in leftist ideology,'" Jewish News Syndicate, September 15, 2022; Joshua Klein, "ZOA Calls to Fire ADL Head after Exposé Reveals 'Dangerous, Extremist Educational Programs,'" The Jewish Voice, September 15, 2022; Daniel Greenfield, "The ADL's Radical Boss Must Go," Frontpage, September 14, 2022. Contents of the exposé can be found in Hannah Grossman, "Anti-Defamation League Launches Review of Education Content after Fox News Digital Investigation," Fox News, September 7, 2022. For the ADL's educational materials, see also its website at adl.org/about/education.

But its doing so remains too weak and too hedged by its countervailing, indulgent, political predilections.

And, once again, the betrayal is not limited to the ADL. As with many Jewish organizations that have joined the ADL in support for Black Lives Matter, a lot of groups, both mainstream and fringe, have expressed support, for example, for DEI programs, despite the central role of such programs in promoting Jew-hatred. In February 2025, as a response to the Trump administration's cutting of DEI initiatives in federal agencies, the Union for Reform Judaism, joined by more than thirty other Jewish groups, released a statement endorsing such initiatives. Even as the statement acknowledged that some Jews see DEI policies as contributing to antisemitism, it argued, in effect, that the inclusiveness supposedly advanced by DEI is too valuable not to salvage, and to reconcile somehow with the protection of Jews, despite the anti-Jewish impact DEI programs have had.[9]

American Jewish Communal Failure and the Israel Scapegoat

The predilection of some members of besieged minorities to embrace the indictments of their attackers, however bigoted or absurd, has other important characteristics. One is that those who do so very rarely acknowledge that they are motivated by a wish to ingratiate themselves with the haters. Rather, they try to cast their stance as impelled by higher ethical aspirations. For example, those who seek to counter the aspersion of Jews displaying a clannishness not seen among other groups, by single-mindedly demonstrating their dedication to broader social causes even at the cost of ignoring threats to the Jewish community, insist their doing so is indeed expressive of a higher moral consciousness. And those who responded to the canard that Jewish engagement in trade was degenerate by endorsing the canard and urging the Jews to give up trade and become, like much of the wider society at the time, farmers, cast their stance, again, not as trying to placate the bigots but rather as promoting the exchange of less savory endeavors for a more wholesome one. (How the farmers would get their goods to market without those engaged in trade was rarely addressed in the context of such moral posturing.)

---

9   See, for example, Ben Sales, "Over 30 US Jewish Groups Sign Letter Defending DEI as an 'invaluable tool,'" *Times of Israel*, February 8, 2025.

Another characteristic of besieged groups embracing the indictments of their besiegers is the predilection to blame some separate part of the community, often a segment across political, social, or religious divides, for supposedly inciting the hatred of the besiegers. Thus, in nineteenth- and early twentieth-century Europe, Jews in German-speaking states commonly blamed Eastern European Jews for inciting Jew-hatred, secular or Reformist Jews tended to blame the more traditionally religious, and socialist Jews blamed the Jewish bourgeoisie as causing antisemitism.

While the great majority of American Jews feel connected to Israel and are supportive of the Jewish state, there is a significant minority that is ambivalent at best with regard to Israel. This ambivalence can be found even more among substantial segments of the Jewish communal leadership. Much of the recent dramatic rise in antisemitism in America has been within quarters with which the largely left-leaning Jewish community feels connected in its fantasy of an immutable alliance. One approach to reconciling the Jew-hatred in those quarters with the delusion of mutual support, an approach beyond simply closing one's eyes to the hatred or rationalizing it as insignificant and marginal, is to construe it as not really directed at the American Jewish community but rather at Israel. Indeed, it is the allure of this tack that is largely responsible for what ambivalence or outright hostility towards the Jewish state does exist among American Jews.

One can see this tack repeatedly at play, for example, within the leadership ranks of Reform Judaism, by far the largest American Jewish denomination in terms of congregations and members. Particularly under the presidency of Richard Jacobs, criticism of leftist sources of anti-Jewish invective has been muted, with such invective commonly interpreted as reflecting a not unreasonable disenchantment with Israel.

Over the last two-plus decades the Israeli electorate has swung markedly to the right. Initially, this happened in response to the failure of the Oslo Accords, torpedoed by Yasser Arafat's rejection of all proposals—including those of then President Clinton—for a final resolution of the Palestinian-Israeli conflict and his unleashing a terror war that claimed more than a thousand Israeli lives. The shift in Israeli voter sentiment was further reinforced by Israel's subsequent unilateral withdrawal from Gaza and the disasters that have followed upon that even prior to October 7, 2023. But the Reform leadership and many of its followers have been critical of the Israeli political landscape and more than prepared to make common cause with much of the anti-Israel sentiment within the American Left.

An example reflective of this is the Reform Movement's declaring three years ago its opposition to the International Holocaust Remembrance Alliance (IHRA) definition of antisemitism being codified in law.[10] As of November 1, 2024, forty-five nations had adopted the definition, including the United States, as well as thirty-seven state governments and ninety-six American county and city governments.[11] But the Reform leadership takes issue with elements of the definition related to Israel. Four organizations within the Reform Movement issued a declaration that states:

> Our commitment to principles of free speech and concerns about the potential abuse of the definition compel us to urge its use only as intended: as a guide and an awareness raising tool. The definition should not be codified into policy that would trigger potentially problematic punitive action to circumscribe speech, efforts which have been particularly aimed at college students and human rights activists.

A Jewish Telegraphic Agency article on the Reform Movement declaration quotes a statement by Reform president Jacobs who expresses his unhappiness with labeling critiques of Israel antisemitic: "I think there is a concerning trend to label groups, including Jewish groups, that are strongly critical of Israeli policy—whether those are policies within the Green Line, whether those are policies in the occupied West Bank—as anti-Semitic, and in a sense demonize those organizations."[12]

But the IHRA definition offers examples of attacks on Israel that it deems antisemitic, and they do not include criticisms of Israeli policies such as those alluded to by Jacobs. Among the IHRA examples are: "Denying the Jewish people their right to self-determination, e.g., by claiming that the existence of a State of Israel is a racist endeavor," and "Applying double standards by requiring of it a behavior not expected or demanded of any other democratic nation."

---

10 "Reform Jewish Institutions Affirm IHRA Working Definition of Antisemitism," Union for Reform Judaism, January 25, 2021.

11 "Adoptions and Endorsements of the IHRA Working Definition of Antisemitism," IHRA, ihra.combatantisemitism.org.

12 Ben Sales, "US Reform Movement: IHRA Definition of Anti-Semitism Should Not be Law," Jewish Telegraphic Agency, January 26, 2021.

Why would the Reform Movement oppose such attacks on Israel being labeled antisemitic? The Reform declaration regarding codifying the IHRA definition in law also states that the definition's Israel examples "must not divert attention from the more frequent manifestations of antisemitism, too often violent, emanating from new streams in the hate movements . . . streams primarily associated with the Far Right."

First, while antisemitism from the Far Right has been growing, is dangerous, and certainly is not to be ignored, it is simply untrue to assert that Far Right Jew-hatred is responsible for "the more frequent manifestations of antisemitism." This was an obviously absurd claim to any unbiased observer before October 7, 2023, and is even more obviously so today. Far Right Jew-hatred, however poisonous and dangerous it is, remains largely marginalized in America. In contrast, leftist antisemitism, as already noted, has penetrated much further into the American mainstream, as has Islamist antisemitism. But much of American Jewish institutional life, and its leaders, identify with left-dominated segments of the society that have become increasingly anti-Jewish and antizionist—again, academia, cultural elites, the mainstream media, social media, elements of the Democrat Party. And major Jewish institutions and their leaders have responded by refraining from calling out the antisemitism of those sources, or by muting their criticisms and choosing to construe anti-Jewish attacks from those sources as really a function of unhappiness with Israel.

The Reform concerns about the IHRA definition of antisemitism being codified in law is a reflection of this perversion of what ought to be the priorities of Jewish institutions. It is overwhelmingly leftist sources of Jew-hatred that promote the extreme bigoted attacks on Israel cited as examples of antisemitism by the IHRA definition. It is leftist sources that the Reform movement chooses to identify with and defend, like the "college students and human rights activists" referred to in the Reform declaration. And the Reform stance then amplifies the betrayal of the Jewish community implicit in this defense of leftist bigots by asserting that it is thereby protecting the community. It is doing so, it asserts, by preventing the calling out of antisemitism being distracted from the supposed main threat, that of the Far Right.

There are many in the Reform movement, including prominent figures such as Rabbi Ammiel Hirsch, who vehemently oppose those who choose to align denomination policies regarding Israel with defamatory and denigrating views of the Jewish state espoused by much of the elite

Left.[13] But cultivating such an alignment continues to be the policy of the denomination's leader and a significant portion of its membership. Beyond choosing to embrace views of the American Left critical of Israel, the Reform leadership has to a large degree also endorsed elements of current leftist cant that is intrinsically anti-Jewish irrespective of positions on Israel. The Reform movement's embrace of DEI orthodoxy, already noted, is discussed by David Bernstein in *Woke Antisemitism*.[14]

One can see where those eager to place an anti-Israel spin on the upsurge of American antisemitism can easily muster superficial support for the claim. Certainly, on the campuses, both within faculties and among students, the focus is overwhelmingly on attacking Israel, and the attacks on Jewish students are justified by the assumption that, unless Jews on campus explicitly demonstrate their own hostility to Israel, they are supportive of the Jewish state. And while among the Democrats in Congress openly antisemitic statements have become more common and more tolerated, the attacks on Israel far exceed the straightforward attacks on American Jews. The same can be said about other bastions of the Left such as mainstream media and elements of the cultural elites.

But for any American Jew to look at this pattern and to accept it at face value, as representing legitimate criticism of Israel and its policies, and, secondarily, as criticism of those who support the Jewish state, would require him or her to ignore the obvious. It would require him or her to ignore that the indictments of Israel—as an apartheid state, a colonial state, or a genocidal state—are such distortions of reality that they are the furthest thing from legitimate criticism. (Of course, one can take issue with specific Israeli policies if they are represented honestly, and while those specific positions may be debatable they would not necessarily be bigoted. But, in fact, very little of the criticism directed at Israel is of this sort.) It would require one to accept the judging and condemning of Israel by standards that are not really standards at all and are invoked with regard to no other state on the planet. It would require ignoring the fact that no Palestinian leader who talks to Western audiences about a two-state solution has ever accepted that one of those states will be the Jewish state of Israel, or the fact that, even as Palestinian leaders call for

13 See, for example, "Ammiel Hirsch: How to Understand Reform Judaism's Anti-Zionist Crisis," 18Forty, July 2, 2024, https://18forty.org/podcast/ammiel-hirsch-how-to-understand-reform-judaisms-anti-zionist-crisis/.
14 David L. Bernstein, *Woke Antisemitism* (New York: Wicked Son, 2022), 112–113.

enforcement of what they claim to be UN resolutions regarding the conflict, they are clearly not prepared, any more than they were in 1947, to accept the realization of the UN partition plan that explicitly called for an Arab and a Jewish state.

It means ignoring the reality that one of the two recent Palestinian governments, that of Hamas in Gaza, has explicitly committed itself not only to the murder of all Jewish Israelis but to the murder of all the world's Jews, and asserted that that commitment is an immutable religious obligation. It means likewise ignoring the fact that the other Palestinian government, the Palestinian Authority, has, since its inception, denied any Jewish historical connection with any part of the land between the Jordan and the Mediterranean, insisting the Jews are merely alien usurpers. It requires ignoring as well that the PA has used all the tools at its disposal, its schools, its media, its mosques, to indoctrinate its people in Jew-hatred and in the necessity of their dedicating themselves to Israel's destruction; that it has used those same tools to drive its people to murder Israelis and has then rewarded the murderers and would-be murderers and their families with generous ongoing "pay-to-slay" cash benefits.

But to point out the above truths is merely to note that those who would cast leftist anti-Israel claims as reflecting "legitimate criticism" of Israel are willfully ignoring the significance of a rhetoric obviously grounded in antisemitism. (It is noteworthy that those Jews who are most ambivalent about Israel and most inclined to find some legitimacy in leftist criticisms are disproportionately Jews who are professionally or in other ways associated with leftist bastions of anti-Israel bias, such as academia, elements of the mainstream media, the progressive wing of the Democrat Party and other elements of government hostile to Israel, as well as elements of the cultural elites.) But the delusion of choosing to comprehend outright hatred and slander of Israel as legitimate criticism goes beyond failing to see that criticism as antisemitic. It also misses the vital point that the attacks on Israel are, in their essence, attacks on American Jews. American Jews are not merely secondary, incidental targets, sullied by association with Israel, as many American Jews would wish to believe. They are primary targets of the propaganda war against Israel.

Islamist/Palestinian assailants of American Jews on the nation's campuses and beyond are certainly haters of Israel and desire its annihilation. But Muslim Brotherhood antisemitism predated Israel and transcended Zionism. Its focus has been to promote its comprehension of Islam's proper place in the world, as the world's exclusive creed and culture, and to promote advancement towards that goal, at least in part, through Jihad. Attacking the Jews, pursuing the objective of their extermination worldwide, the acknowledged intent of Hamas, has been embraced as religiously required and strategically useful. It is useful for discrediting and undermining those in the Arab and broader Muslim world who seek cooperation with a Jew-tolerating West. And it is useful in helping divide and weaken the West by demonstrating Jihadi power against a vulnerable Western-allied minority and by sowing internal division and discord and undermining Western resistance to Islamist penetration. Hamas leaders have stated on a number of occasions that the pursuit of Israel's destruction is only a small part of the organization's intent and that its ultimate end is Islamic domination of the entire world.[15] If there were no Israel, Islamist antisemitism would still thrive. And, again, the Islamist hatred of Israel is in large part derived from the perception of the Jews as the weakest and most despised of peoples (and at the same time the most satanically powerful) and their reestablishment of their national home in the middle of the Muslim world as, therefore, the most intolerable insult to the proper order of things.

A vivid illustration of how the Islamist/Palestinian anti-Israel campaign in America views American Jews as primary targets, and of how its antisemitism transcends connections to Israel, was provided in 2022 by the Boston Mapping Project, an undertaking of BDS supporters in Massachusetts and beyond. The Project created a map of Jewish organizations in the greater Boston area. It also included industrial, academic, and law enforcement sites to which the Jewish organizations supposedly have nefarious links. It provided street addresses for many of the organizations, and stated that its aim: "in pursuing this collective mapping was to reveal the local entities and networks that enact devastation, *so we can dismantle them*. Every entity has an address, every network can be disrupted" (emphasis added).

The Project goes on to encourage people to use the map for advancing "resistance in all its forms," presumably including violence. Among the Jewish entities pinpointed on the map are religious sites, schools, an artist collaborative, a disability group, and unions. The Project also names some individuals:

---

15   See, for example, "Hamas Reiterates Goal of World Domination by Islam—Annihilation of Israel—Establishment of Caliphate in Jerusalem," Militant Islam Monitor, March 28, 2007, https://www.militantislammonitor.org/article/id/2790.

community philanthropists, other community leaders, and board members of some organizations.

The Project, in offering links to non-Jewish organizations such as law enforcement bodies and industries, seeks—as it explicitly states—to indict the American Jewish community for being a promoter and enabler of law enforcement's supposed racism, of imperialism and colonialism, of capitalist exploitation. This broadbrush attack, like the general inclusion of Jewish communal entities of any sort, clearly transcends the issue of Israel and resembles Soviet antisemitic propaganda, while the Boston Mapping Project's all but explicit call for violence against the Jewish community converges with white supremacist and neo-Nazi agendas in America. It is noteworthy that the Goyim Defense League, a white supremacist group focused on promoting antisemitism, praised the Mapping Project as "super, duper, ooper important."[16]

The current antisemitism purveyed by Black radicals on campuses and by some Black groups and organizations derives even less from concerns about Israel and Zionism. Is the key genuinely, as the Black Lives Matter organization, its Congressional followers, and the intersectionality crowds on the campuses, assert, about Palestinians being people of color and Israelis being white—itself an absurd and counter-factual distinction? If that were the case, then identification with Hamas would be more than outweighed by the reality of Hamas's Middle East and African Islamist allies being responsible for countless atrocities against people of color. They have murdered literally millions of Black Africans and enslaved hundreds of thousands more over the last half century—Christians, Muslims, and followers of local religions. The anti-Israel animus would be more than countered by the reality that many of the Black African nations victimized by Islamist terror have turned to Israel for help in fighting the onslaught.

A much more realistic appraisal of Black antisemitism in recent decades is provided in the articles by Henry Louis Gates, Jr., cited in Chapter One.[17] Again, Gates notes that a recent survey had shown Blacks twice as likely as Whites to hold antisemitic views and "that it is among the younger and more educated blacks that anti-Semitism is most pronounced." This was, and

---

16 Cited in "Boston Mapping Project: An Anti-Semitic Campaign Goes Awry," Committee for Accuracy in Middle East Reporting and Analysis, July 19, 2022. (Much of the above discussion of the Mapping Project is drawn from this source.)
17 Gates, Jr., "The New Black Anti-Semitism is Top-Down and Dangerous."

continues to be, a reflection of the antisemitism promoted by the heirs of the 1960s and 1970s Black radicals and by groups like the Nation of Islam. As Gates points out, it is antisemitism in the service of advancing both sources' radical, often separatist and supremacist, agendas, much like the Far Left's antisemitism has been in the service of advancing its Marxist agenda. That more educated Blacks have also been exposed to, and influenced by, the antisemitism of the professors and the campuses has only exacerbated this trend of greater antisemitism particularly among the so-called educated elite.

Gates also writes:

> But why target the Jews? . . . The answer requires us to go beyond the usual shibboleths about bigotry and view the matter, from the demagogues' perspective, strategically: as the bid of one black elite to supplant another . . . It requires us, in short, to see anti-Semitism as a weapon in the raging battle of who will speak for black America—those who have sought common cause with others or those who preach a barricaded withdrawal into racial authenticity . . . The strategy of these apostles of hate, I believe, is best understood as ethnic isolationism: They know that the more isolated black America becomes, the greater their power . . . And what's the most efficient way to begin to sever black America from its allies? Bash the Jews, these demagogues apparently calculate, and you're halfway there . . . Many American Jews are puzzled by the recrudescence of black anti-Semitism, in view of the historic alliance between the two groups. The brutal truth has escaped them: that the new anti-Semitism arises not in spite of the black-Jewish alliance but because of that alliance.

The same is true of the Far Left, progressive/Marxist, wing of the Red-Green-Black alliance, in academia and beyond, which has always targeted Jews as a way of advancing its class warfare agenda and weakening the societies it wants to overthrow. It is largely the antisemitism directed towards American Jews that is primary, the targeting of Israel secondary.

This can be seen clearly in, for example, the Far Left, progressive promotion of critical race theory (CRT) and the agenda of progressive "diversity, equity and inclusion" (DEI) programs in grade schools, colleges, and universities as well as myriad institutions beyond the realm of academics. The pattern closely follows that dissected by Gates with regard to the strategy of Black radical circles. The CRT and DEI agenda is to advance division between favored minorities, on the one hand, and White Americans and disfavored minorities, on the other. American life is presented as a zero sum game, where anything accrued by Whites and other communities among the disfavored is at the expense of the favored. The CRT and DEI programs are driven by advocates who perceive themselves as a new elite trying to displace and destroy the integrationist elite in the United States along with their allies. For them, attacking Jews is a useful tool in this struggle. First, Jews are considered as not a favored minority, and—even worse—as white, and so antisemitism is not a concern and should not be a concern to those dedicated to CRT and "diversity, equity, and inclusion." Worse still, Jews have always been overwhelmingly aligned with the integrationist elites—the point Gates makes—and, so, demeaning and otherwise attacking Jews, even demonizing them, serves to undermine advocacy of the integrationist vision. It serves as well to tar those who share that vision, whether Whites and disfavored minorities or those members of favored minorities who do so. And one can find attacks on Jews recurring in, for example, proposals for mandatory DEI curricula in various grade school settings across the nation. While that targeting may mention Israel and Zionism, it clearly entails attacks on American Jews unrelated to Israel.

Yet many in the American Jewish community, and a large proportion of its leadership, prefer to close their eyes to this reality and to insist that, if Israel were only more accommodating of the Palestinians, then the antisemitism of the Palestinians/Islamists, the Black radicals, and the progressives/Marxists would recede and all would be well. It is the mindset captured in that article by Gary Rosenblatt cited in Chapter One and entitled "Frustration with Israel is Growing Here at Home."

But such self-delusions come at a price. Today's plague of rampant antisemitism in America cannot be effectively countered if its sources and its objectives—particularly the role and the aims of the Red-Green-Black intersectionality alliance, American society's most pervasive and mainstreamed font of antisemitism—are not honestly recognized and forcefully challenged and fought by a unified Jewish voice, not a fractured one.

Chapter Four

Self-Delusions and the Modern Diaspora

———

"Stunned by the hailstorm of anti-Semitic accusations, the Jews forget who they are and often imagine that they are really the physical and spiritual horrors which their deadly enemies represent them to be . . . The Jew is often heard to murmur that he must learn from the enemy and try to remedy the faults ascribed to him. He forgets, however, that the anti-Semitic accusations are meaningless . . .

Max Nordau, 1897[1]

"It is the greatest triumph of anti-Semitism that it has brought the Jews to view themselves with anti-Semitic eyes."

Max Nordau[2]

In the early modern period, Jews commonly responded to any indictments coming from the wider society by seeking communal reform to accommodate the attackers, or by detaching themselves from the Jewish community

---

1   Max Nordau, speech to the First Zionist Congress, in *The Zionist Idea*, ed. Arthur Hertzberg (New York: Harper, 1959), 235–241. Citation is from 241.
2   Cited in Meir Ben-Horin, *Max Nordau, Philosopher of Human Solidarity* (New York: Conference of Jewish Social Studies, 1956), 180.

in order to rid themselves of the communal taint. By the mid-nineteenth century, Jews consistently perceived politically conservative forces to be in general less amenable, and liberal forces as more open, to giving civic rights to Jews. They then gradually came to focus upon the latter as the group whose anti-Jewish critiques they took to heart and whom they sought to appease via communal reforms. Later events, particularly the rise of fascism in Europe between the two world wars and its widely accompanying, and ultimately genocidal, antisemitism, reinforced among Jews this perception of the Right as hostile and the Left as potentially less so.

This, in broad strokes, is the political background of the pattern noted in the previous chapters. Even today, American Jewish leaders and much of their constituencies consistently focus on antisemitism emanating from the Far Right and ignore, downplay, or seek to pursue the path of ingratiation in response to Jew-hatred coming from the Left or its partners in the Red-Green-Black alliance, even as the assault from the latter has penetrated much more into the American mainstream.

Early Modernity: Indictment and Self-Indictment

Central European states began considering the issue of granting civic rights to Jews in the late eighteenth and early nineteenth centuries. Those opposed to providing such rights pointed to specific characteristics of the Jews that ostensibly rendered them unfit. As noted in Chapter Three, whatever indictment was offered of the Jews in this discussion, however bigoted or outrageous, there were invariably people inside the Jewish community who endorsed the charges. They were driven by the wish to believe that the proffered criticism was the main stumbling block on the road to civic equality, and that Jewish reform to accommodate the indictment would undo the animosity. They desired to have, and to exercise, some control over circumstances that cast a shadow over their lives, even though in reality they had no such control. Most broadly, the pattern of self-indictment was fueled by an eagerness to believe, despite experience to the contrary, that life was fair, that people were fair and rational, that irrational, unmitigable hatred did not exist. Consequently, antisemites must have some basis for their bigotry in their experience, and the right counter-experience could appease them.

Among the popular antisemitic indictments in Central Europe at the time was the claim that Yiddish was a crude, bastardized, unwholesome language that reflected the degenerate nature of the Jews and illustrated their unfitness for citizenship rights. Many Jewish leaders and members of the Jewish cultural elite embraced this assessment of Yiddish and condemned it as, in the words of one such figure, "a language of stammerers, corrupt and deformed, repulsive to those who are able to speak in a correct and orderly manner."[3] And, "I am afraid that this jargon has contributed more than a little to the immorality of the common man."[4] Both quotes are from Moses Mendelssohn, a man who adhered throughout his life to devout Jewish religious practice and who dedicated himself to promoting the well-being of fellow Jews. His sharp denigration of Yiddish reflected his wanting to believe that the Jews' language was a major source of anti-Jewish bias and that abandoning Yiddish would go far towards ending that bias.

Jews were also criticized at the time for being primarily engaged in trade. Such work was interpreted as another mark of their degeneracy, further rendering them inappropriate for citizenship. This, too, won the endorsement of some Jews. Indeed, a major effort of the *maskilim*—the devotees of Haskalah, the Jewish Enlightenment—was to encourage and even force Jews to cast off their supposedly reprehensible endeavors and take up more wholesome occupations like farming and the crafts. This, it was thought, would make Jews more worthy of their neighbors' acceptance.

Some gentile observers, even early in this period, offered much more positive assessments of Jewish involvement in commerce. The English playwright and essayist Joseph Addison, writing in the *Spectator* early in the eighteenth century, opined that,

> [The Jews] are, indeed, so disseminated through all the trading parts of the world, that they are become the instruments by which the most distant nations converse with one another, and by which mankind are knit together in a general correspondence: They are like the pegs and nails in a great building, which, though they are but little valued in themselves, are absolutely necessary to keep the whole frame together.[5]

---

3   Moses Mendelssohn, cited in Sander L. Gilman, *Jewish Self-Hatred* (Baltimore, MD: Johns Hopkins University Press, 1986), 102.

4   Cited in Michael A. Meyer, *The Origins of the Modern Jew* (Detroit, MI: Wayne State University Press, 1967), 44. Meyer writes, "Psychologically there seems to be a trace of self-hate or simple shame in Mendelssohn's strange reasonings" with regard to Yiddish.

5   Cited in Lucy Dawidowicz, *What is the Use of Jewish History?* (New York: Schocken, 1992), 252.

American statesman George Mason, who was a prominent delegate to the Constitutional Convention and played an important role in framing the Bill of Rights, likewise viewed Jewish engagement in trade in positive terms. The Jews, he wrote, are "not only noted for their knowledge of mercantile and commercial affairs, but also for their industry, enterprise and probity."[6] But such perspectives were rare in Central Europe. What the Jews heard there were predominantly derogatory, disparaging assessments of their endeavors, and all too often—like the abused child embracing his or her inferred comprehension of what it means to be "good" or "bad" as having transcendent validity—they chose to embrace those attacks as reflecting some transcendent truth and as answerable only by Jewish reform.

In the course of the nineteenth century, Jews in substantial numbers abandoned Yiddish as their primary language and switched, for example, to "good" German. These were primarily Jews who had moved from former Polish territories that had been annexed by Prussia and Austria to elsewhere in Prussia, to other German-speaking states, or to the German-speaking areas of the Habsburg empire. There were also some Jews from Polish areas seized by Russia who managed to migrate westward to German-speaking lands. Significant segments of the community also succeeded in leaving behind the commercial occupations of their fathers to become poets, composers, philosophers, and intellectuals of various other stripes.

Many leading voices in the surrounding society then argued that Jews might gain command of the German language, or master German poetic or musical forms or the subtleties of German philosophy, but they could not discard their alien Jewish minds and sensibilities. Such voices maintained that Jews were still unable to apply their learning to true aesthetic or intellectual creativity but instead were subverting what they had learned to some lesser, alien end. Even this indictment was embraced by some in the Jewish community, who insisted Jews were indeed being too pushy in their cultural endeavors and that most people who took part in these endeavors were, in fact, introducing alien and lesser "Jewish" elements that were coarsening German culture.

Perhaps the best-known expositor of this view was the Austrian Jewish writer Karl Kraus.[7] Born in 1874, Kraus spent his adult life in Vienna pursuing a writing career that brought him unique prominence as a satirist and as a

---

6   Cited in Lipset and Raab, *Jews and the New American Scene*, 13.
7   See, for example, Harry Zohn, *Karl Kraus* (New York: Twayne, 1971).

social and political critic. The major vehicle for his writing was the widely read journal *Die Fackel* (The torch), which he founded in 1899 and edited until his death in 1936. Kraus declared his estrangement from the Jewish community in 1898 and converted to Catholicism in 1911. Nevertheless, throughout his career he was attacked as a Jewish writer, indeed often as the quintessential Jewish writer, supposedly using an alien and corrupt Jewish literary language and stylistic mode to disseminate equally alien and corrupt Jewish ideas. Kraus in turn focused his critical and satirical assaults on other Jews, accusing them of being the true purveyors of an alien, Jewish literary language and style and of alien, Jewish ideas. Among Kraus's targets were Theodor Herzl, the writers Hermann Bahr, Arthur Schnitzler, and Felix Salten (author of *Bambi*), as well as various Jewish newspaper editors and reporters.

Kraus acknowledged that by racial definition he was a Jew. But he consistently chose to believe that the anti-Jewish animus directed against him and so prominent in the larger society was actually inflamed by faults that were alien to him, the faults of the people he was targeting. He also chose to embrace much of that animus as deserved and even wrote that his Jewish targets were precipitating the "destruction of Austria by Jerusalem." Other statements by Kraus that in tone and content mimicked the antisemitic press include: "Jew boys are the poets of a nation to which they do not belong"; "the inevitable pogrom of the Jews against ideals"; his depiction of Austria as "a state which had the most corrupt Jewish influences circulating in its veins"; and his declaration that "*Gemütlichkeit* and Jewishness" were "the driving forces of Austrian decay."[8]

Kraus's writings convey his obvious if futile desire to separate himself in the public eye from what was popularly seen as Jewish. They also convey his belief that, if Jews embraced sufficient self-reform and divested themselves of what he argued were their negative cultural, linguistic, and intellectual attributes, they would indeed overcome the surrounding society's anti-Jewish hostility. Kraus insisted that the gentile antisemites did not really mean much of what they said, and he seems to have believed that they posed no real threat to the Jews. It was only with the rise of Nazism in Germany and the burgeoning of Nazi influence in Austria (again, Kraus died in 1936) that he began to rethink his anti-Jewish assumptions.

Even the most virulent racist attacks on the Jews, arguments that the Jews' alien, inferior, and dangerous nature is essentially immutable and that neither

---

8   Cited in Zohn, *Karl Kraus*, 38 and 41.

conversion nor any other attempts by Jews to better themselves can have any salutary effect, had their Jewish defenders. Such indictments of the Jews very early became a major element in the arguments of the Jew-baiters. In the latter part of the nineteenth century, with the emergence of a new pseudo-science of race and racial studies, the notion of the inherently alien and inferior nature of the Jew became an even more prominent and established concept in German political discourse and popular belief. And some Jews incorporated the concept of racial inferiority into their image of Jews and of themselves as Jews.

The figure most often cited as an example of this phenomenon is another Austrian, Otto Weininger. Weininger was born in Vienna in 1880, into a liberal, assimilated family. His father was a renowned goldsmith who produced muse-um-quality art objects. Otto's sister later wrote of their father: "[He] was highly anti-semitic, but he thought as a Jew and was angry when Otto wrote against Judaism."[9] The father apparently approved when Weininger converted to Christianity in 1902, and the rest of the family subsequently converted as well. Also in 1902 Weininger earned his doctorate from the University of Vienna.

A year later he published *Sex and Character*,[10] a work based on his university studies and devoted largely to arguing and documenting the supposed inherent inferiority of women, also a pseudo-scientifically buttressed and widely popular concept at the time. For example, according to Weininger, women are consti-tutionally devoid of genius, dignity, and morality. But Weininger also devotes a section of his book to the Jews and argues that Jews are intrinsically even more limited than women. Here he repeats many of the old, if at times mutually contradictory, canards against the Jews: They are incapable of higher forms of thought; they lack aesthetic sensibility; they are materialistic; they are commu-nists who lack an appreciation of property; they are excessively emotional. But, in regurgitating these old attacks, Weininger invokes elements of the new racial science and the idea of genetically transmitted racial character.

How did Weininger see himself? In other writers of Jewish origin who endorse the concept of supposedly inherent negative Jewish traits, such as Karl Marx, there appears to be a cognitive disjuncture through which they somehow exempt themselves from what they declare to be universal and inescapable. But this was not true of Weininger. On the contrary, he seems to pride himself on consciously recognizing the same racial traits in himself and hating them in himself as he does in others. Weininger writes:

---

9   Cited in Robert Wistrich, *The Jews of Vienna in the Age of Franz Joseph* (Oxford: Littman Library, 1989), 519.
10   Otto Weininger, *Sex and Character* (New York: Howard Fertig, 2003).

> The bitterest anti-Semites are to be found amongst the Jews themselves . . . [But] only the commoner natures are actively anti-Semitic and pass sentence on others without having once sat in judgement on themselves in these matters; and very few exercise their anti-Semitism first on themselves. This one thing, however, remains nonetheless certain: whoever detests the Jewish disposition detests it first of all in himself; that he should persecute it in others is merely his endeavor to separate himself from Jewishness; he strives to shake it off and to localize it in his fellow-creatures, and so for a moment to dream himself free of it.[11]

But, Weininger suggests, he himself is too self-aware and too honest to entertain such a dream. Weininger was familiar with Sigmund Freud's writings and, in fact, tried to interest Freud in his own work. Here, he applies Freud's concept of "projection"; that is, the attributing to others negative characteristics one perceives in oneself, as a way of defending oneself against the negative self-perception.[12]

In the context of the psychodynamics of besieged communities, one might indeed, like Weininger, comprehend as projection that some members of such communities accept the attackers' indictments but see others in the community (rather than themselves) as embodying the derogatory ascriptions. An example would be Jews who are inclined to perceive other Jews as fitting

---

11 Ibid., 304.
12 Freud's first published use of the term in this context was in a discussion of the psychodynamics of paranoia in "Further Remarks on the Neuro-Psychoses of Defence" (1896). See *The Complete Psychological Works of Sigmund Freud*, trans. and ed. James Strachey (London: Hogarth Press, 1962), vol. 3, 162–185, 184.

Anna Freud, in her comprehension of identification with the aggressor as having its original expression in a virtually universal childhood embrace of parental criticism. saw projection as playing a role in the evolution of this defense mechanism. She, and many subsequent psychoanalysts who have written on identification with the aggressor, have widely noted the subject's projecting the painful self-indictment—the embrace of the aggressor's criticism—onto others. They direct at others the same criticism and become the aggressor, thereby further "mastering" the indictment and reinforcing the sense of rapport with the subject's own attackers. For Anna Freud, such projection was an early stage of identification with the aggressor, when the individual eschews taking the indictment to heart by redirecting it toward others, with embrace of the indictment being a further developmental step. She also observed that some people remained stuck in projecting the aggression and never moved to the next step. See Anna Freud, *The Ego and the Mechanisms of Defense*, esp. 119.

antisemitic caricatures. But Weininger did not regard the antisemitic characterizations of Jews as caricatures. For him, they were accurate, immutable depictions. And, again, he saw himself as rather unique in readily, honestly, applying those depictions to himself. Weininger committed suicide a year after appearance of his book, at age twenty-three. His death has been widely linked to his inability to come to terms with what he hated in himself but could not exorcize, what he perceived to be the immutable Jew within him.

Some scholars, including Robert Wistrich, have suggested that Weininger's Jew-hatred was, like his misogyny, a product of his disturbed sexuality rather than a reflection of social and political stresses. With regard to misogyny, Weininger himself attributed it generally, as he did Jewish antisemitism, to projection: "Hatred of women is always only an unmastered hatred of one's own sexuality."[13] But even if Weininger's antisemitism was founded on a self-loathing of psychosexual origin, the general point regarding the readiness of abused minorities to embrace the indictments of their abusers still stands. The social and political predicament of an abused group, of Jews, for example, facing the wider society's claims that they are damaged and inferior, fosters not only straightforward absorption of the criticism. It also inclines its victims to associate any sense of inadequacy and taint, of whatever origin, with their group identity.

All the examples of Jewish absorption of anti-Jewish indictments discussed above were propelled by the Jews' desires to appease their attackers. However biased and absurd the indictments, some Jews invariably took them to heart and urged Jewish self-reform, or even self-abasement, in the delusional hope of thereby winning relief.

"Jewish Self-Hatred"

The Austrian Jewish writer and early Zionist Max Nordau was not alone in recognizing the phenomenon of Jews seeing themselves "with antisemitic eyes." In the early twentieth century a literature evolved on the subject of what was widely labeled "Jewish self-hatred." The term captures an essential reality concerning Jews' sense of themselves as individuals when living under conditions of duress. For example, a Jewish child subjected at school

13   Cited in German in Wistrich, *The Jews of Vienna*, 524, n. 108 (translation by the present author).

to constant taunts, social exclusion, even physical attacks, will very often respond by questioning what is wrong with him and how can he change to win acceptance. This response is comparable to that of the child abused at home. If the Jewish child's parents and community fail to convey a strong enough counter-message, such a response becomes virtually inevitable and will likely be carried by the child into adulthood, with the child as adult feeling himself tainted and flawed by virtue of his Jewish identity.

A case study in this phenomenon is offered by Theodor Lessing, a German Jew who published a book entitled *Jewish Self-Hatred* in 1930. The analyses of self-hatred in such writings were often based at least in part on their authors' own experiences, which is also true for Lessing. In another work, an autobiography entitled *Once and Never Again: A Life's Memories*, he offers a vivid picture of someone who had followed the course of, by his own subsequent lights, "self-hatred" and had finally "healed" himself.

According to Lessing, he knew virtually nothing of his Jewishness growing up:

> At home nothing was spoken of Judaism. There was no longer any Jewish observance in the family . . . For the youth of Hanover, the word Jew was an invective . . . and I innocently went along with this. In the third grade of elementary school there were, in addition to me, two Jewish children, Sussapfel and Ransahoff. Sussapfel was always first in the class. Ransahoff, a large, weak boy, was always attacked. Children are cruel, and I also tormented poor Ransahoff, until one day, when I called him a "Jew," he answered, "You're also one." I responded indignantly, "That's not true." But I asked my mother, what is a Jew. She laughed and gave an evasive answer. Once, however, she pointed out in the street a man in a kaftan and said, "That is a Jew."
>
> From this I concluded that we were not the genuine thing. But the word Jew remained sinister to me. As I childishly absorbed all the many national and religious prejudices of the school, and had no counterweight at home, I thought that Jew is something evil.[14]

---

14 Theodor Lessing, *Einmal und nie wieder* (Guetersloh: Bertelsmann Sachbuchverlag, 1969), 112 (translation by the present author).

Lessing earned doctorates in medicine and philosophy, wrote extensively on philosophy and the history of ideas, and pursued a successful teaching career in Hanover, where his family had lived for more than three centuries. In the post-World War I period, however, he recognized that efforts by Jews such as himself to divest themselves of their Jewish identity and make themselves into Germans did nothing to ameliorate the anti-Jewish animosity of those around them or its rationalizations and pseudo-justifications. He observed in *Jewish Self-Hatred*, in the context of the recent Arab massacres of Jews in Mandate Palestine and the growing strength of the antisemitic Right in Germany:

> It was said: "You are parasites in foreign places," so we tore ourselves loose from where we lived. It was said: "You are middlemen among the peoples." So we brought up our children to be farmers and cultivate the land. It was said: "You are degenerating and becoming cowardly weaklings." So we went into battle and became the best soldiers. It was said: "You are everywhere only tolerated." We answered: "We know no deeper longing than to move beyond being objects of tolerance."
>
> However, when we chose to preserve our distinctiveness [as a people] then it was said: "Have you still not learned that this tenacious preservation of your separate peoplehood is treason against all universal human values?" We answered in that, after a hundred dead and wounded, we quietly disbanded the Jewish Legion. We gave up our self-defense and placed our proper rights under the protection of the European conscience. And what is the result?[15]

By the time he published his book on Jewish self-hatred, Lessing had reconnected with a Jewish identity and become an ardent Zionist and articulate writer on Zionism. He also wrote attacks on the Nazis and, with the Nazi seizure of power, was forced to flee Germany. He and his wife moved to Marienbad in Czechoslovakia. But the Germans posted a bounty on them and, in August 1933, Lessing was murdered by Nazi assassins.

---

15 Theodor Lessing, *Der Judische Selbsthass* (Munich: Matthes and Seitz Verlag, 1984), 10–11 (translation by the present author).

"Jewish Antisemitism"

There are limits, however, to the utility of the concept of "self-hatred" in characterizing Jews' embrace of anti-Jewish indictments. For one, it has the weakness of painting with too broad a brush what are, in fact, a range of responses among Jews in the face of chronic attack. Consider a community of Jews living under such assault and those within the community who are inclined to take to heart the surrounding society's indictments. Some will seek to escape their Jewish identity, to distance themselves entirely from a community that they see as bearing the ugly taints that the haters ascribe to it. They will perhaps convert to the dominant religion and strive to adopt fully the identity of the society's dominant group. Others will continue to feel a bond to the Jewish community, maybe even assume leadership positions in it, and dedicate themselves to reforming their fellow Jews in conformity with the indictments of the surrounding society. Both groups, by accepting the indictments as truth, manifest "self-hatred." But they do so in markedly different ways, with radically different objectives, and with what is likely to be a dramatically different impact on their community of origin.

A greater problem with the concept of "self-hatred" is its masking of the fact that Jews who embrace anti-Jewish canards as truth seem more often to see other Jews rather than themselves, or more than themselves, as fitting the anti-Jewish caricature. Their response to Jew-hatred in surrounding societies is manifested more as hatred of other Jews than "self-hatred."

For example, in the nineteenth and early twentieth centuries, German Jews commonly viewed Eastern European Jews as the true targets of the antisemites and reason for Jew-hatred. At the same time, secular Jews blamed the more traditionally religious, and socialist Jews blamed the Jewish bourgeoisie. Nordau could have said that, if Jews had come to see themselves through antisemitic eyes, they were even more inclined to see other Jews that way, particularly Jews on the other side of political, religious, and social divides. This reality has led some writers on the subject to prefer the term "Jewish antisemitism" over the older "Jewish self-hatred."

One can argue that the predilection of many Jews to see Jews on the other side of political, religious, or social divides as the true targets of the antisemites and the ones fitting the antisemitic caricatures does not necessarily mean that the term "self-hatred" is inappropriate. That predilection may simply be an expression of "projection" as discussed earlier; these people, in hating other Jews, may simply be trying to defend against the self-hatred within them. No

doubt, there is some truth to this. Lessing, for example, looks back at his earlier criticism of other Jews, particularly Eastern European Jews, and himself
characterizes his earlier behavior as an expression of self-hatred. An example
of that earlier behavior is his account of a trip to former Polish territories in
1906. In it, Lessing echoes antisemitic caricatures of Polish Jews: They are
filthy, corrupt, degenerate, and hypocritical in their piety. He discussed his
trip in newspaper articles which were ostensibly about the effects of political
repression on Eastern Jews, but his focus was on the allegedly ugly nature of
Polish Jewry. Lessing's writings in this vein elicited a reproach for his bigotry
from, among others, Thomas Mann, a non-Jew.[16]

But the broad generalization—that hating other Jews, particularly Jews
across political, social, religious divides, can almost invariably be construed
as a projection of self-hatred—presents difficulties. There may well have been
people who felt so alienated from the majority of Jews—those "other" Jews—
and felt so comfortable in their personal assimilation, or the assimilation of
the particular subset of Jews with whom they identified, that they genuinely
did experience little if any "self-hatred" in response to what antisemitism they
saw around them.

A closely related problem concerns other premises that underlay the broad
application of the concept of "self-hatred." Some Jews, in response to the
increasingly pervasive and shrill anti-Jewish content of German social-politi-
cal discourse, concluded that there was something shamefully demeaning in
Jewish efforts to take on a German identity and win an acceptance that clearly
was not possible. This perspective contributed to the rise of the early literature
on "Jewish self-hatred." Its authors saw the wider society's hostility as evidence that efforts to attenuate a Jewish identity and subsume it to a German
one were intrinsically pathological, a sick self-abnegation that could only end
in disappointment, disorientation, and self-loathing. However, their view of
efforts to shed one's Jewish identity as inexorable violence to one's essential
self was clearly an overstatement. If those German Jews who perceived their
Jewish identity as primarily a burden and sought to suppress it subsequently
experienced distress and some modicum of self-loathing, they did so in large
part because their efforts were widely met with rebuff. They were in turmoil
because much of the larger culture told them that they remained Jews no matter what their desires and efforts to become German, and not simply because
the quest to cast off their Jewishness was intrinsically anxiety-producing and

16   See Solomon Liptzin, *Germany's Stepchildren* (Cleveland, OH: Meridian, 1961), 165.

disorienting. Moreover, some people found their way to a new identity open, perhaps because they hid their origins successfully. They encountered in their personal experience a greater willingness among those around them to regard them as they wished to be regarded. Many of them—particularly if they had been reared with an already attenuated Jewish identity—likely experienced very little angst, psychological disequilibrium, or fractured sense of self; they shed their Jewishness without ever looking back.

The emergence of a literature on Jewish self-hatred was accompanied by, and helped foster, other writings that offered a more positive view of Eastern European Jewry. They presented Eastern Jewry as in many respects more centered, more whole, and more wholesome, its members often enjoying a psychological integrity that compared well to the fractured and conflicted sense of self that seemed to characterize the assimilating Jews of the West. This theme was most notably developed by Martin Buber. Not all those writing about Jewish self-hatred in the West shared this view of Eastern Jewry. But some writers, including Hans Kohn, Josef Prager, and E. J. Lesser, did. Their papers on the subject, discussed by Sander Gilman in *Jewish Self-Hatred*,[17] all appeared in Buber's journal *The Jew*.[18]

Those Jews who looked at other Jews through "antisemitic eyes" not only parroted Jew-baiting cant but also typically judged other Jews by standards they applied to no other group. The Jewish American political theorist and commentator Walter Lippmann, scion of a wealthy German Jewish family and perhaps the most influential American news columnist in the years between the world wars, repeatedly echoed popular anti-Jewish indictments in his writing and blamed Jews for the hatred directed against them. Ronald Steel, in his acclaimed biography of Lippmann, notes with regard to one such assault on the Jews published in 1922:

> The crudeness, even the cruelty, of Lippmann's attack on his fellow Jews was in dramatic contrast to the sensitivity he had shown to other minority groups and to individuals suffering discrimination or poverty. It was inconceivable that he would

17 Sander Gilman, *Jewish Self-Hatred* (Baltimore, MD: Johns Hopkins, 1986), 297–298.
18 On the history of this positive view of Eastern Jewry among some German Jews, see Steven E. Aschheim, *Brothers and Strangers: The East European Jew in German and German Jewish Consciousness, 1800–1923* (Madison, WI: University of Wisconsin Press, 1982), especially 100–214.

have written anything comparable about, for example, the Irish, the Italians or the blacks . . .[19]

The reason for this double standard, the explanation for Lippmann's crude anti-Jewish writings, is clear. Lippmann was eager to distance himself from other Jews, to respond to the anti-Jewish bias in the surrounding society by declaring, in effect: Yes, you're right about the Jews, I agree with you; but I'm different from the rest of them and don't share their taint, and so I am worthy of your acceptance.

While this phenomenon of Jews endorsing the anti-Jewish indictments of surrounding societies became more prominent with the weakening of Jewish communal institutions, it has, in fact, been a constant element of the Jewish response to besiegement throughout the history of the Diaspora. Almost inevitably, some members of the community would embrace aspects of the anti-Jewish animus of the surrounding society, choose to believe that the hostility was based on the lamentable behavior of some subset of the community, and harbor wishful expectations that Jewish self-reform would end the hatred. For example, the twelfth-century Jewish traveler Benjamin of Tudela wrote about the Jews of Constantinople:

> Among [them] there are craftsmen in silk and many merchants and many wealthy men . . . They dwell in a burdensome exile. And most of the enmity comes about because of the [Jewish] tanners who make leather and fling their filthy water into the streets at the entrance to their homes, polluting the street of the Jews. And therefore the Greeks [Constantinople was at the time, of course, still in Byzantine hands] hate the Jews, whether good or bad, and make their yoke heavy upon them and beat them in the streets.[20]

The historian H. H. Ben-Sasson observes of this passage:

> This information certainly did not reach [Benjamin of Tudela] from the tanners; it was how wealthy Jews explained

---

19 Cited in Ronald Steel, *Walter Lippmann and the American Century* (Boston, MA: Little, Brown, 1980), 192.
20 Cited in H. H. Ben-Sasson, "The Middle Ages," in *A History of the Jewish People*, ed. H. H. Ben-Sasson (Boston, MA: Harvard University Press, 1976), 385–723.

to themselves and to others the animosity of the Greeks towards the Jews. It resulted from the filthy habits of those who followed such a despicable craft, and because of them all Jews, good and bad, suffered. In this context "good" meant the silk-maker or physician, and "bad" meant the miserable tanner, blamed as the source of this animosity.[21]

The besieged Jews chose to ignore the actual roots of the hostility directed against them, about which they could do little. Instead, they focused their resentment on elements within the Jewish community on the other side of the social-occupational divide. They chose to believe that, if these others were "reformed," it would radically ameliorate the community's predicament.

It was hardly uncommon for some Jews in pre-modern times, living under the duress that was consistently the fate of Diaspora communities in both Christian and Muslim worlds, to blame others within their community for the Jews' plight, or to abandon the community, convert, and join the Jews' oppressors. But such steps seem to have been much less common (excluding episodes of forced conversion) than might be expected given the Jewish predicament. The explanation lies in strong Jewish institutions that reinforced a sense of ongoing meaningfulness, viability, and mission and gave form to longings for ultimate redemption.

These institutions went beyond simply religious structures. They entailed structures that reinforced a sense of nationhood and indeed helped Jews to function as a quasi-national community. Perhaps the most alien for us to grasp from a modern perspective, and perhaps also the most powerful force for securing Jewish continuity, was the institution of Jewish autonomy.

A Brief History of Jewish Autonomy

In ancient times, even after the suppression of the second Jewish rebellion in Eretz Israel in 135 CE, Jews continued to exercise extensive self-governance under Roman rule. The Sanhedrin and the Jewish Patriarchate were soon reestablished in the Galilee and assumed wide civil as well as religious jurisdiction over the surviving Jewish community of Eretz Israel. The Diaspora communities generally acceded to the authority of the Galilee leadership

---

21   Ibid., 469.

and paid taxes to support it. In addition, imperial governments typically leaned toward recognizing the powers of the new Jewish leadership and even enforced its taxing rights in both Eretz Israel and the Diaspora. The Patriarchate and the Sanhedrin retained civil and religious authority and continued to levy taxes even when their official recognition was withdrawn. Indeed, Jewish autonomy in Eretz Israel under the Patriarchate endured for more than a century after the establishment of Christianity as the imperial religion, ending only at the initiative of Theodosius II around 425.

There also existed in Roman times, of course, a large Mesopotamian Jewish community, which traced its origins to the Babylonian Captivity after destruction of the First Temple in 586 BCE. This region was now under the sway of a Persian people, the Parthians. The Jews of Mesopotamia and adjoining Parthian territories constituted the largest Jewish community outside of Roman dominion and likewise enjoyed a high degree of autonomy in civil and judicial as well as religious matters. Its leaders were the exilarchs, who were regarded as descendants of the House of David and accorded the rank of high royal officials by Parthian kings.

In the seventh century, Muslim conquerors destroyed the Persian Empire (then ruled by the Sassanians, another Persian people who had succeeded the Parthians) and seized control of large swathes of what had been Byzantine territory. Those Jews living in the conquered regions who were spared the severer treatment meted out by Muslim authorities won their exemptions largely because they provided what their new rulers valued as useful services. In such circumstances, they were also accorded elements of autonomy.

The granting of extensive autonomy to Jews in return for services rendered to rulers developed most formally in Western Europe beginning in the eighth century. With the Arab seizure of North Africa and Spain in the late seventh century, the Christian realms of Western Europe lost their traditional Mediterranean trade routes. This loss was exacerbated by the frequent hostility of Byzantine rulers toward Western Christian states. Jewish communities in the south of France subsequently grew in importance as contacts between them and Jewish centers in Muslim territories served to reestablish trade routes. These Jewish communities became the major trade bridge between the Christian West and the East. From the latter half of the eighth century, under Charlemagne and his successors, and in response to the new importance of the Jews in international trade, and increasingly in local trade as well, Jewish communities were given charters entailing rights of settlement, trading concessions, regime protection, and self-government. This became the model for legal organization of the Jewish presence in medieval Western European states and ultimately in Eastern European states as well, as Jews later moved eastward from Central and Western Europe.

Jewish self-government extended to most areas of civil and even criminal jurisprudence. It provided effective control over the civil as well as religious life of the community. Even members' employment fell within the aegis of Jewish autonomy, and not just in terms of community leaders setting and enforcing standards for vocational practice. Leaders also determined to a large extent who was allowed to practice particular vocations and with whom among other Jews or among the surrounding gentile population they could do business. (For example, the Jewish leadership often established and enforced measures that prevented competition among community members. This was not simply a Jewish practice; the concept of the normality and appropriateness of vocational competition is a modern one. Medieval guilds, which excluded Jews and worked to eradicate Jewish competition, also had as a central function overseeing the practices of their members so as to preclude competition among them.)

This wide authority meant that Jews experienced the reality of Jewish peoplehood in practical terms every day. Moreover, this autonomy was conferred by rulers who viewed the Jews as a distinct community; it was an expression of that understanding. And so Jews saw their peoplehood not only as continuing to have practical meaning but as having its meaningfulness acknowledged by the highest authorities in the surrounding societies.

In addition, Jews experienced Jewish autonomy as essentially positive, and not just in the sense of protecting Jews from the difficulties they would likely have endured had they been, in civil and criminal matters over which they had autonomy, subject instead to the jurisdiction of the surrounding societies. Jews perceived their situation as, despite the social constraints, disabilities, and abuses to which they were subjected, preferable in various practical respects to the life of most people around them, indeed in some respects privileged by virtue of their relationship with their realm's secular elites. The eminent Jewish historian Salo Baron observed in this regard that "medieval Jews at their worst were better off, both politically and economically, than the masses of villeins who usually constituted the majority of each European nation."[22]

---

22 Cited in Ismar Schorsch, *From Text to Context: The Turn to History in Modern Judaism* (Hanover, NH: Brandeis University Press, 1994), 384–385.

Jews likely did not regard these positive practical circumstances as due simply to individual talents. Rather, they associated their situation with being part of an autonomous community whose leadership had established, and now sustained for its members, the practical advantages they enjoyed. That is, they perceived what was positive in their lives as emanating from their membership in the Jewish community.

Jewish autonomy gave a very tangible rebuttal to assertions that Jewish nationhood had ceased to exist, or to exist in any positive sense, with the loss of Jewish national independence and the rise of Christianity as the successor faith. Administered by a leadership that included sages and teachers who assured Jews of their ongoing place in history and of their ultimate redemption, autonomy gave additional weight to those spiritual assurances.

Jewish autonomy could not, however, safeguard the Jews against physical depredations. Rulers invited Jews into their realms, extended protection to them, and granted them autonomy in return for services they derived from the Jews, but there was an obvious fragility to this arrangement. A ruler could decide that the Jews were no longer useful to him or, more commonly, that their use was outweighed by other considerations. Still, looking particularly at medieval Europe, rulers' usual action then was not physical assault but revocation of charters and exile.

Physical assault most often occurred at times when a ruler's authority was compromised to a point where other elements in the society hostile to the Jews, often clergy and their followers, could attack them with impunity. Indeed, it was characteristic of this period, in contradistinction to later centuries, that assaults on the Jews—including the extensive slaughter associated with the First Crusade, lesser assaults connected with later Crusades, and the widespread murderous attacks related to the Black Death—were almost invariably instigated from below, by lower clergy, marauding armed bands, or town burghers, in defiance of rather than in accord with the policies of heads of state. On a number of occasions rulers executed leaders of the Jews' assailants. The phenomenon of governments initiating and choreographing assaults on the Jews—seen not only in Germany during the Nazi era but throughout eastern Europe between the world wars, and in czarist Russia and Romania in the late nineteenth and early twentieth centuries, and in Communist Russia, and, later, in Communist Eastern Europe—is largely a modern development. It was very much the exception to the rule during the medieval era.

Moreover, during the Middle Ages, when rulers decided that political prudence required them to rid themselves of "their" Jews, there were almost invariably other sovereigns in other realms who saw profit to be had by inviting the Jews to immigrate. And these other rulers would typically extend to the immigrants wide-ranging rights and privileges, including broad autonomy, as enticements to their coming and as protection both of the Jews and of their own interest in them. There was no medieval precedent for the situation that prevailed during the rise of Nazism or during the Nazi slaughter of the Jews, when anti-Jewish sentiment was so widespread and so rabid that almost no country offered the Jews refuge.

The largest medieval Jewish communities in Europe, and the richest expression of Jewish self-governance, evolved in Spain between the ninth and the fourteenth centuries. The next peak occurred after the general dissolution of Western European Jewish communities and the eastward migration of Jews, in Poland and the merged Polish-Lithuanian state. The model of medieval Jewish self-governance, and with it the strongest of Jewish communal institutions, effectively came to an end with the loss of Polish independence in the late eighteenth century, at which point Polish Jews numbered about 800,000 and constituted by far the largest Jewish community in the world and at least a third of all surviving world Jewry.

More on Early Modernity: Self-Indictment in the Guise of Progress

In the eighteenth century, there remained only vestigial Jewish communities in Central and Western Europe. Some had survived beyond the Middle Ages, as in parts of Italy and in some German states. Others were reestablished after earlier expulsions, as in France and England. But they had all been stripped of their medieval rights or were reestablished without such rights. For example, among decrees promulgated by Friedrich the Great of Prussia concerning Jews in Prussia in 1750 was the explicit declaration that the authority of rabbis and community elders would be strictly confined to religious matters and that "[the rabbis and community leaders] shall not presumptuously undertake to make any real decision and settlement of a case in matters of secular law, for the rabbi and the elders have no right to real jurisdiction. On the contrary, matters must be referred to the proper court of justice."[23]

---

23 Cited in Jacob Rader Marcus, *The Jew in the Medieval World* (Cincinnati, OH: Hebrew Union College Press, 1990), 76.

The end of Jewish autonomy was part of broader political developments. In this period, European nation states of all stripes—both despotic and democratic—sought to centralize power under a national bureaucracy and to strip all relevant groups of vestiges of chartered rights handed down from the medieval era. This effort was directed at such groups as the nobility, clergy, and municipal burghers as well as the Jews. But for Jews, the weakening of communal institutions left community members more vulnerable to the psychological corrosiveness of persistent besiegement by surrounding societies—the ongoing marginalization, denigration, and at times physical attack.

In Eastern Europe, Prussia, Austria, and Russia, which took control of former Polish and Lithuanian territories, chose largely to isolate these territories and not integrate them or extend to them fully their own national structures. This arrangement allowed some continuation of earlier Jewish communal institutions. In addition, the vacuum created by the weakening of older institutions—whose earlier strength had derived from their chartered rights in Poland and their rapport with Polish leaders, most notably the landed nobility—was filled to some extent by new communal organs created by the Hasidic movement and its leaders or, particularly in former Lithuanian areas, by the leadership of strengthened traditional yeshivas. But older as well as newer establishments had very limited ability to advocate for the Jewish community with the new controlling powers.

In czarist Russia, the government consistently pursued policies that harassed and impoverished the Jews in the newly acquired areas and was impervious to Jewish efforts to win relief. The absence of any substantive rapport with the authorities rendered both old and new leaderships incapable of tending to their communities' needs with sufficient effectiveness. The concept of Jewish nationhood and the positive evaluation of Jewish identity remained alive in the East to a far greater degree than in the West, due largely to the more recent experience of autonomy in the Polish-Lithuanian state. But the inability of the community's institutions to address adequately people's needs in the face of czarist hostility translated into a decline in their authority. This, in turn, led to a lessening of those institutions' ability to inspire and to provide a counterweight to the psychological corrosiveness of the Jews' besiegement.

That corrosiveness, and the embrace by Jews of the indictments of their tormentors, can, again, find various modes of expression. Some will try to reform themselves, and perhaps their community, to address the indictments. Some will see elements of the community that are in some way different from themselves as the true carriers of the taint and either seek to reform those others or focus on distancing their own segment of the community from those others. Some will simply disassociate themselves from the Jewish community in an effort to divest themselves of the Jewish taint. And some will join with the Jews' attackers to establish their escape from the taint even more emphatically.

But whatever the particular path taken by those Jews who embrace the indictments of Jew-haters, a noteworthy common aspect is that they typically cast their stance not as an effort to assuage anti-Jewish attitudes but rather as reflecting some higher moral or ethical position. For example, those who criticized Jewish involvement in commerce typically argued that there was indeed something intrinsically reprehensible in commercial endeavors and morally superior in other types of employment.

Similarly, in response to claims by anti-Jewish voices that the Jews were only interested in their own well-being, pursuing solely their own parochial agendas, Jews often aggressively sought to avoid focusing on the needs of the Jewish community, even as the community suffered disabilities that were unique to it. Such Jews strove instead to enlist in broader causes, and they would cast their doing so not as an attempt to assuage accusations of parochialism but rather as a righteous emphasis on broader social needs.

In a related vein, another indictment by people who sought to deny Jews citizenship rights was that the Jews were a separate nation and so should not be absorbed as equal citizens. One Jewish response to this occurred within Reformist congregations that were founded by Jewish communities in the German states. These congregations often chose, among other accommodations, to expunge longings for Jerusalem and a return to Eretz Israel from the Jewish liturgy as a means of demonstrating that Judaism entailed a purely religious and not national identity. Those who advocated such reforms did not cast their doing so as an effort to appease anti-Jewish opinion but rather as representing a progression of the Jewish faith toward an exclusively universal ethical message and mission. In this context, any longing for return to Zion was stigmatized as narrow-minded and atavistic.

Again, the predilection to frame embracing the perspectives of the haters as somehow choosing a morally superior path is consistent with a pattern discernible in abused children. Such children's images of becoming "good" are clearly driven by fantasies of pleasing their abusers in a manner that will win relief. However, they typically comprehend what constitutes their being "bad" and what it would mean to reform and become "good" as representing transcendently meaningful ethical and moral choices.

Categorical Thinking

One can argue that attempts by minorities to accommodate the wider society can and do at times succeed in winning them greater acceptance. That such an outcome can occur is, of course, true; and, for example, Jewish exertions to give up Yiddish and master normative German can be perceived as a pragmatic step. But that is very different from endorsing the derogation of Yiddish as intrinsically primitive, inferior, and corrupting. Such endorsements were founded on the desire to believe that Jews were regarded with distaste and loathing and treated as inferior because they spoke an inferior language and had been coarsened by it. Becoming linguistically equal to their neighbors, then, would assure their being treated as equal—a wish-driven delusion.

Similarly, it was not unreasonable that Prussian Jews, at the time of Prussia's struggle against Napoleon, might look to demonstrations of patriotism as positive, pragmatic steps toward winning the acceptance of the surrounding society. But note the more wishfully definitive expectations contained in a call to arms issued by two leaders of the Berlin Jewish community, Eduard Kley and Siegfried Gunsburg: "There upon the battlefield of honor . . . where all work for a single goal: for their fatherland...there also will the barriers of prejudice come tumbling down. . . . Hand in hand with your fellow soldiers you will complete the great work; they will not deny you the name of brother, for you will have earned it."[24]

In fact, from 1813 to 1815, seventy-two soldiers from the small Prussian Jewish population won the iron cross; fifty-five Prussian Jewish officers died at Waterloo.[25] Nevertheless, as has so frequently happened, the Jews in post-Napoleonic Prussia faced hostile political and social forces that transcended anything they as a community did or did not do.

These last examples reflect a propensity for "categorical" thinking—that is, choosing to see communal policies in the face of anti-Jewish bias in black and white terms, to believe particular Jewish reforms will assure acceptance by the surrounding society and failure to reform will assure ongoing hostility. Of course, any reforms to promote acceptance would more realistically be understood as, at most, pragmatic steps that may or may not have positive consequences. The propensity for black and white, or categorical, thinking on such matters is driven, again, by the desperate desire for acceptance and,

---

24   Cited in Meyer, *The Origins of the Modern Jew*, 139.
25   Ibid., 139.

consequently, by wishful self-conviction that acceptance could inexorably be won by the right communal policies. It is the communal equivalent of the abused child's wishful belief that his being "good," taking the right actions, will assuredly win him relief. A similar mindset can be seen in other communal stances as well.

For example, Central European liberals—some on the basis of principle, others for pragmatic reasons—were generally more receptive to the extension of rights to Jews than more conservative elements. But in aligning themselves with liberal groups, many Jews chose not to recognize that this sympathy was at least partly driven by a convergence of political interests that could change in the future. Instead, in their desperation for support and for opportunities to diminish Jewish vulnerability by linking their fate to broader, and more powerful, social identities, they wishfully construed the link with liberal parties as having transcendent significance and endurance. Likewise, they chose to see the liberals as the force that was certain to shape the future.

Gabriel Riesser was a leading German Jewish liberal activist in the mid-nineteenth century and almost unique among Jewish political activists at the time in his vocal and energetic pursuit of the cause of Jewish legal equality. It was most common for Jews who entered politics in the German states to strive aggressively to separate themselves from Jewish issues and even from their Jewish identity.

But Riesser, too, eschewed any position that would appear too parochially Jewish and wishfully linked the Jews' fate to presumably sympathetic broader forces. Thus, he repeatedly articulated stances that subsumed the problem of Jewish disabilities to more general political and nationalist matters and put unbounded faith in liberal support. Riesser declared at one point: "Give me Jewish equality in one hand and the realization of the beautiful dream of Germany's political unification [primarily a liberal objective at the time] in the other . . . and I will unhesitantly choose the latter, for I am convinced that unification also encompasses equality."[26]

The extent to which many Jews chose to idealize the connection with German liberals and the fruits of Jewish self-effacement is captured in an exchange between Riesser and the conservative German academic and theologian H. E. G. Paulus. Paulus argued that, as long as Jews adhered to their religion, they constituted a separate nation and were entitled to be protected

---

26 Cited in Shmuel Ettinger, "The Modern Period," in *A History of the Jewish People*, ed. H. H. Ben-Sasson (Boston, MA: Harvard University Press, 1976), 727–1096, esp. 830.

subjects in Germany but not full citizens. Paulus also suggested that the Jewish push for full integration as Germans would end in their expulsion or even extermination. Riesser responded that German unification would inexorably be built on liberal Enlightenment principles of justice and equality and so would inevitably entail the granting of full equality to the Jews.[27]

The issue is not that Riesser proved so catastrophically wrong. It was not impossible that events could have unfolded very differently and more in keeping with his hopes. The point is his willful, self-deluding certainty, despite much countervailing evidence, that the right Jewish alliances and self-effacements would inevitably yield the results he desired.

Identification with the Left

Jews' categorical identification with parties of the Left became commonplace throughout Central and Western Europe. It was driven both by a desire to avoid what might be condemned as Jewish particularism and by wishful thinking that embedding Jewish aspirations in larger movements could assure Jewish well-being. For some, this identification went beyond liberal parties to socialist and communist groups.

In Germany and elsewhere in Central and Western Europe, most Jews sought to be like their neighbors, to win acceptance by fitting in. They tended to subscribe to mainstream liberal political thinking. Of those who embraced socialism, many did so because they had become disenchanted with the liberal parties, which provided, for example, no bulwark against *de facto* discrimination and the rise of antisemitic political parties in the wake of German unification in 1871. Some Jews hoped that in immersing Jewish concerns in the struggle of other disadvantaged groups, particularly the working class, and in seeking a more radical restructuring of society, they might win relief from persisting Jewish disabilities. Some hoped in particular that, if the Jews distanced themselves from the bourgeoisie and the excoriated Jewish link with the middle class, many of their enemies would be mollified. Other Jews in Western Europe embraced Far Left parties in an effort to divest themselves of a Jewish identity entirely, assuming the alternative identity of champion of the working class.

---

27 "Gabriel Riesser," *Encyclopedia Judaica* (Jerusalem: Ketem Publishing, 1972), vol. 14, 166–169; esp. 167.

Marx and Lassalle

Illustrative of that latter group is the godfather of modern communism, Karl Marx. Marx's father had converted to Christianity about a year before Marx's birth, at least in part to advance his career, and had thereafter cultivated a German cultural identity. The elder Marx appears to have regarded his path as having abandoned a lesser identity for a superior one and to have encouraged the same perspective in his son, whose conversion he arranged when the boy was six.

From his earliest entry into the public arena, Karl Marx was clearly interested in distancing himself from "the Jews." In the words of the historian and philosopher Isaiah Berlin: "[Marx] was determined that the sarcasms and insults, to which some of the notable Jews of his generation, Heine, Lassalle, Disraeli, were all their lives a target, should, so far as he could effect it, never be used to plague him."[28] The persistent heat of his anti-Jewish diatribes suggests that, when Marx continued to be the target of anti-Jewish barbs, he chose to blame not his tormenters but rather "the Jews" for casting the shadow of their tainted existence over his life, and he responded by striving even harder to separate himself from them.

In his writings, Marx both parrots and elaborates upon the popular anti-Jewish argument that the Jews' involvement in trade is evidence of their degeneracy, as well as the further claim that Jews are incapable of genuine aesthetic or intellectual achievement. In his essay "On the Jewish Question" (1844), he argues that the Jewish mind is too limited and Jewish thinking too concrete to have fashioned a true religion. Instead, it produced a pseudo-religion whose practical expression is materialism and occupation in trade. Also as a consequence of their limited nature, the Jews lack a capacity for creativity and aesthetic sensibility. Marx writes in the essay, "What is the worldly cult of the Jew? Huckstering. What is his worldly god? Money . . ."[29] That which is contained in an abstract form in the Jewish religion—contempt for theory, for art, for history, and for man as an end in himself—is the real, conscious standpoint of the man of money."[30] Moreover, according to Marx, to the

---

28   Isaiah Berlin, *Karl Marx: His Life and Environment*, 4th ed. (Oxford: Oxford University Press, 1978), 73.

29   Karl Marx, *Early Writings*, trans. and ed. T. B. Bottomore (London: McGraw-Hill, 1964), 34.

30   Ibid., 37.

degree that money has become the basis of the social order in the West, the West has been Judaized. "The god of the Jews has been secularized and has become the god of this world."[31] From this perspective, the radical agenda becomes for Marx not just a transformation of modern society to bring about the liberation of everyone, including the Jews, but rather a transformation of modern society whose essence will be a liberation of the world from the ethos of the Jews. Variations on the same anti-Jewish themes are a feature in Marx's writings throughout his life.

One can see in Marx's published anti-Jewish arguments more than an attempt to distance himself from the Jews in the public eye. His arguments are also a retort to those critics who, in their attacks on his writings, characterized them as ill-conceived products of the alien, primitive, and malevolent Jewish mind. (By 1850, there were already published attacks on Marx in an antisemitic vein, casting him as a revolutionary determined to impose a Jewish dictatorship on the German world. Such attacks continued throughout his life.)[32] Marx insists that the defenders of the status quo, of bourgeois society, are themselves "Judaized" and have united with the Jews to hinder human development.

This tack of Jews or Jewish converts responding to antisemitic invective against them by insisting that their critics are themselves behaving like "Jews" recurs throughout the nineteenth century. For example, Heinrich Heine, another convert, was subjected to arguments from critics that his poetry was inexorably marred by the aesthetic limitations and lack of artistry characteristic of the Jewish mind. Heine retorted that his critics, by engaging in excited, fantastical arguments against him, were themselves emulating the primitive Jewish ways of Talmudic disputation instead of more measured and reasoned critical discourse.

But, however much Marx's gentile critics were a target of his arguments, those arguments remain, of course, crude assaults on the Jews. They regurgitate and amplify the popular canards of contemporary Jew-baiters. And Marx's ultimate aim in employing them was to gain credibility by demonstrating his separateness from "the Jews."

The phenomenon of Jews joining the Jews' vilifiers was not limited to the most radical among those who have sought to exchange a Jewish identity

---

31 Ibid., 37.
32 Frank E. Manuel, *A Requiem for Karl Marx* (Cambridge, MA: Harvard University Press, 1995), 20.

for a socialist or communist one. Ferdinand Lassalle, both less radical and less given to obsessively spewing anti-Jewish rants than Marx, nevertheless reflected in his career a similar course. Lassalle was a founder of the German labor movement, first president of the General German Workers Association, and a major spokesman for socialism in the German arena. His break with the Jewish community seems to have been driven in large part by temperament and ambition, but it also entailed some absorption of the broader society's anti-Jewish animus. At the age of sixteen, Lassalle writes in his diary of imagining himself a Jewish military hero, and he expresses distaste for what he sees as the Jews' passivity in the face of their tormentors.[33] He returns to this theme in later years, articulating his alienation from the community and the faith, but his later comments also clearly include attempts to assure others of his distance from the Jews and reflect his embrace of popular anti-Jewish canards. He writes at one point:

> I do not like the Jews at all, I even detest them in general. I see in them nothing but the very much degenerated sons of a great but vanished past. As a result of centuries of slavery, these people have acquired servile characteristics, and that is why I am so unfavorably disposed to them. Besides, I have no contact with them. There is scarcely a single Jew among my friends and in the society which surrounds me [in Berlin].[34]

Lassalle had ambitions that—given his time and place—could not be fulfilled while he remained within the Jewish community. This apparently made him all the more open to embracing the anti-Jewish bigotry of the surrounding society. He never converted or denied his Jewish origins, and he could even joke at himself in his anti-Jewish remarks, as when he wrote: "There are two classes of men I cannot bear; journalists and Jews—and unfortunately I belong to both."[35]

The broader palette Lassalle chose was the German labor movement and socialism. Lassalle complained at times of the passivity of German workers, in statements resembling his comments about Jewish passivity. But that did not

---

33 Robert S. Wistrich, *Revolutionary Jews from Marx to Trotsky* (New York: Harper and Row, 1976), 7–8.

34 Ferdinand Lassalle, *Une Page d'amour de Ferdinand Lassalle* (Leipzig: Brockhaus, 1878); Gilman, *Jewish Self-Hatred*, 205.

35 Cited in Wistrich, *Revolutionary Jews*, 57.

compromise his sensitivity to the workers' plight as a disadvantaged and abused population in German society or his energetic and often courageous championing of their predicament, not just as a writer and theoretician but as activist organizer. In contrast, the adult Lassalle was more inclined to embrace the canards cast at the Jews than to take offense at the abuses and disabilities heaped on them.

Moreover, in his championing of German labor and socialism, Lassalle himself introduced anti-Jewish themes as he attacked middle-class liberalism. For example, he wrote of the Jewish editor of the liberal newspaper *Berliner Volkszeitung*, "A man who cannot even write German but is slowly but surely corrupting our nation's language and its character with the peculiar gibberish with which he feeds his readers—that so-called Jewish-German."[36]

No doubt, some of those who sought to shed their Jewish identity and immerse themselves in an alternative identity as socialist or communist brothers-in-arms with the downtrodden working class succeeded in being accepted as they wished. But what drove them was still largely a delusion, a wish to believe that embracing the anti-Jewish indictments of the surrounding society and associating themselves with one faction of the indicters would inexorably end their being seen as Jews and spare them the arrows shot at "the Jews." Reality, of course, is not subject to such inexorable control.

It was not simply that the radicals' opponents commonly labeled these people Jewish agents of a nefarious Jewish agenda. Even within the ranks of the radical Left, and certainly among much of its working-class constituency, Jewish radicals were often still identified with the Jewish community more broadly as unreformable capitalist enemies. And even among those fellow radicals who were relatively free of anti-Jewish biases, the radical universalism so common among the former Jews, their dismissal of all ethnic, cultural, and national distinctions as insignificant, atavistic, to be discarded in the future radical utopia, was commonly viewed as a particularly Jewish vision of the socialist future. And indeed so it was, born of those Jews' eagerness to discard and render insignificant their own ethnic connections.

A later example: in early twentieth-century Germany, the scholars of the Frankfurt Institute for Social Research were largely deracinated Jews who had embraced the Marxist creed as the essence of their alternative identity. Those among them who managed to escape Nazi Germany had typically,

---

36 Wistrich suggests that Lassalle's anti-Jewish rhetoric in attacking middle class liberals was a major inspiration for his successors in the leadership of German socialism and the German labor movement, who prominently employed antisemitic themes. However, antisemitic rhetoric was already popular in the German Left.

before being obliged to leave, dismissed the rising antisemitism. It clashed with their neo-Marxist analyses of the dialectic of history, their conviction that human history is explicable entirely in terms of conflicts based on class, and their insistence on the essential inconsequentiality of religious and ethnic affiliations. They chose to regard German antisemitism as an insignificant phenomenon unworthy of their scholarly attention. The Jews of the Frankfurt Institute, in their flight from Jewish identity, created another identity readily recognizable as that of fleeing Jews. Thus, in a droll characterization of the Institute, renowned Jewish scholar Gershom Scholem called it one of the "most remarkable 'Jewish sects' that German Jewry produced."[37]

The Jewish Left in Eastern Europe

In the late eighteenth century, when Poland was divided among Russia, Prussia, and Austria, Russia gained the most territory, including control of Warsaw, and thereby dominion over by far the largest Jewish population in the world. In response to czarist depredations, a number of Russian Jews, like some among their Western coreligionists, fled their Jewish identity to recast themselves as socialist champions of their nation's downtrodden elements, and joined various radical Russian groups. But, as noted earlier, in Eastern Europe during the nineteenth century Jews retained more of a national consciousness and more robust communal institutions than elsewhere. One consequence was that Russian Jews also formed parties of the Left that were specifically Jewish, a phenomenon virtually unknown in the West. Russian Jewish socialist parties included, for example, the Bund, which was antizionist, as well as a number of socialist Zionist groups.

But, in Russia as elsewhere, Jews who affiliated with the socialist parties commonly took to heart anti-Jewish assaults on the Jewish bourgeoisie. They tended to view both the Jewish middle class and traditionally religious Jews as the true targets of Jew-haters, while their own path was progressive and future-oriented and provided an escape from the shadow of antisemitism.

Illustrative are the writings of Russian Jewish novelist and essayist Joseph Hayyim Brenner. Brenner early in his life became involved with the Bund but

---

37 Cited in Barry Rubin, *Assimilation and Its Discontents* (New York: Times Books, 1995), 148. On the Frankfurt Institute for Social Research, see also Paul Connerton, *The Tragedy of Enlightenment: An Essay on the Frankfurt School* (Cambridge: Cambridge University Press, 1980).

later shifted his loyalties and exertions to socialist Zionism and ultimately moved to Eretz Israel. (He was murdered in Tel Aviv by Arab assailants during the May 1921 wave of Arab terror.) The following excerpts are from his 1914 essay entitled "Self-Criticism":

> The mode of our living . . . is not one that does us great honor. . . . Yes, we may exist as a mass of gypsies, peddlers, traveling salesmen, and bank clerks. . . . Who can tell us whether, had there been no universal and understandable hatred of such a strange being, the Jew, that strange being would have survived at all? But the hatred was inevitable. . . . It would be a sign of steadfastness and power, of productive strength, if the Jews would go away from those who hate them and create a life for themselves . . . If there is no great [such] movement today, if only a handful of young men can be found among twelve million to give their sweat with which to rinse off the horrible plague of huckstering that has infected us, and their calloused hands to roll our historic shame off our backs—then this is a sign, the sign of Cain, that the hucksters cleave to their huckstering because they lack the strength for anything better.
>
> Then come our national apologists and tell of the steadfastness of the Jews in their religious belief. But what value is there for us in our ancestors' practice of some religious customs, particularly those that cost no money, in the hope of being rewarded in the world to come? . . . Those hundreds of generations lived not on Sanctification of the Name, but on various schemes aimed at fulfilling, for their own benefit, the commercial functions demanded of them by the general populace; they lived to safeguard their money and increase the interest rates, and also—to guard themselves against baptism. But concessions in religious matters to the demands of the external environment were never lacking. . . .
>
> We never had workers, never a real proletariat . . . Our urge for life whispers hopefully in our ear: Workers' Settlements, Workers' Settlements. Workers' Settlements—this is our revolution. The only one.[38]

---

38   Joseph Hayyim Brenner, "Self-Criticism," in *The Zionist Idea*, ed. Arthur Hertzberg (New York: Harper and Row, 1959), 307–312.

Throughout Europe, those Jews who supported socialism while retaining a sense of Jewish identity tended to ignore or even give some credence to the intense anti-Jewish rhetoric that was almost everywhere an element of socialist cant. As for Jews who embraced socialism as an alternative identity and sought to shed any link to the Jewish community, they often contributed to anti-Jewish socialist rhetoric, as illustrated in the earlier citations from Marx and Lassalle.

In the late nineteenth and early twentieth centuries, European Jews who suffered from chronic besiegement and had imbibed elements of the anti-Jewish indictments to which they were subjected, brought these perspectives with them to Eretz Israel. The dominant group in the Yishuv—the Jewish community in Eretz Israel—and the leaders of the Zionist project were socialist Zionists from Russian-controlled territories, many of whom shared Brenner's views. European Jewish immigrants also brought those perspectives with them to America.

Chapter Five

Jews in America: The Psychological Scars of Besiegement Transplanted

---

"As an American Jew and Zionist, I am deeply ashamed of the reference to you in the Palestine Resolution adopted by the Republican National Convention. It is utterly unjust, and you may be sure that American Jews will come to understand how unjust it is."

> Rabbi Stephen Wise, leader of the American Jewish Community, writing to
> President Roosevelt about the Republican Party adopting, in June 1944, a strong
> pro-Zionist plank in its platform for the upcoming election and criticizing
> Roosevelt for not pressing Britain to open Mandate Palestine to
> Jews trying to escape Hitler.[1]

In the first decades of the twentieth century, Jewish immigrants to America—particularly those from Eastern Europe, where the vast majority of recent immigrants originated—gave some support to American socialist parties. But with the presidency of Franklin Roosevelt Jews became overwhelmingly aligned with the Democrat Party. The embrace of the Democrats was motivated by pragmatism as well as principle. At a time of intense antisemitism in America, starting soon after World War I and exacerbated by the socially corrosive effects of the Depression, Jews suffered expressions of bias that affected their basic

---

1   Cited in Rafael Medoff, *The Deafening Silence* (New York: Shapolsky, 1987), 178.

capacity to function in the society. As historian and rabbi Arthur Hertzberg noted of this period, "Almost no Jew could make a free, personal decision about his education and career. At every turn, the fact of his Jewishness meant that many, if not most, options were simply not available to him."[2] The public employment and other programs Roosevelt introduced as part of the New Deal were largely open to Jews at all levels and broke with the prevailing blackballing of Jews. In addition, the Jewish predilection to immerse Jewish objectives in broader social agendas, and to pursue rapprochement with the disadvantaged as a means of winning greater acceptance, converged with Roosevelt's building of his grand Democrat alliance of the underprivileged.

At the same time, evident during these years are delusional elements similar to those we saw at work in Jewish communities in Europe. Just as in the Old World, they reflect Jewish vulnerability and attempts to find relief through the embrace and accommodation of anti-Jewish canards. These elements include acceptance of the indictment of "parochialism," a conviction that relief could inexorably be won by demonstrating the opposite, and a predilection to characterize avoiding anything that might be seen as "parochial"—which often meant failing to address vital communal interests—as actually reflecting a higher ethical commitment to broader social agendas. Also, in America, as in Europe, Jews indulged in wishful thinking that pragmatic and possibly transient alliances can represent transcendent and enduring convergences of interests and goals, and consequently were blind to changes in the political landscape and slow to respond to them.

With the rise of the Nazis in Germany, and even with the revelation, in late 1942, of the Nazis' program to exterminate all of Europe's Jews, these elements of Jewish political life in America compromised the American Jewish community's response. To be sure, effectively promoting the rescue of Jews from Europe was difficult in the face of the prevailing anti-Jewish attitudes and, more particularly, the hostility of the State Department. Still, the major step in this direction—the creation of the War Refugee Board (WRB) in early 1944—happened primarily through the efforts of a small group of Jews acting outside the mainstream Jewish leadership. (The key activists were the so-called "Bergson group" led by Hillel Kook from Mandate Palestine, who adopted the pseudonym Peter H. Bergson during his sojourn in the United States as a Zionist emissary affiliated with Ze'ev Jabotinsky's Revisionist camp.)

---

2   Cited in Rubin, *Assimilation and Its Discontents*, 86.

The War Refugee Board succeeded, despite persistent administration obstruction, in contributing to the rescue of an estimated one hundred and fifty to two hundred thousand Jews. About ninety percent of its funding came from Jewish charities, as the administration not only largely refused to cooperate with its efforts but also withheld financial support for which it was eligible. The WRB's substantial achievements were no doubt far less than they would have been had it had the government support mandated in the executive order that created the agency.

Its successes included its office in Turkey getting about 7,000 Jews out of the Balkans and ultimately into Mandate Palestine. The Turkish office also successfully negotiated the transfer of the 48,000 Jews still alive in Transnistria into the interior of Romania and the provision of effective measures for their security there. The WRB's Swiss office was able to move money across the Swiss border to underground forces in Nazi-occupied areas for the rescue, hiding, and care of Jews. It is estimated that at least 10,000 Jews survived largely because of this program.

The WRB also lent its support to two efforts by European Jewish leaders to convey to the Germans that the Allies were secretly considering a German offer to exchange a million Jews, mainly from Hungary, for 100,000 trucks, ostensibly to be used only on the Eastern front. (In fact, the British rejected the offer and refused to go along with those urging that, rather than sending a message of outright rejection, they at least hint at Allied interest in order to buy time and some interim protection for those Jews still alive. According to British documents, British officials were concerned that any show of interest might "lead to an offer to unload an even greater number of Jews onto our hands.")[3] The WRB-backed ruse seems to have been responsible for saving some 15,000 lives. The Nazis, to demonstrate their own continued interest in the proposal, transported nearly 1,700 Hungarian Jews to Switzerland. Another 18,000 were sent to a labor project in Austria rather than to Auschwitz, with three-quarters of them surviving the war.[4]

Finally, in June 1944, the WRB arranged through the head of its Swedish office to have Raoul Wallenberg go to Hungary. Wallenberg, working as, in effect, the WRB's representative in Hungary but with the authority and the cover of a Swedish diplomatic appointment, aggressively issued

---

3   Cited in David S. Wyman, *The Abandonment of the Jews* (New York: Pantheon, 1984), 244.
4   Ibid., 245.

protective Swedish papers and provided safehouses to more than 20,000 Jews.[5] Wallenberg was also instrumental in mobilizing other neutral legations to extend protection to Budapest Jews and played what appears to have been a crucial role in preventing the final liquidation of the Budapest ghetto and its 70,000 inhabitants.

Again, the WRB came into being largely through the efforts of a small group of Jews acting outside the mainstream leadership. Although the Jewish leadership did try to promote rescue, its exertions were compromised both by fear of an anti-Jewish backlash and by its loyalty to Roosevelt. Some mainstream Jewish leaders worried that their advocacy of rescue would be viewed as Jewish parochialism and lack of patriotism in a time of war. For example, throughout the Nazi era the American Jewish leadership avoided campaigning for increasing Jewish immigration to the United States out of concern about igniting still greater anti-Jewish sentiment.[6] This concern, however, was often cast as reflecting not a fear of antisemitic responses but a morally correct eschewing of particularist objectives. (It was very often non-Jews who led the way in asserting that the Nazi assault on the Jews was not just a Jewish issue but a crime against humanity.)

Roosevelt's Indifference to Jewish Plight

Key elements of the Jewish leadership were averse to criticizing Roosevelt, even though it was very clear that he could have saved large numbers of people at minimal political cost to himself and that he was at best indifferent to the plight of Europe's Jews. Simply insisting that the State Department stop erecting additional barriers to the issuing of visas and to the use of visas that had already been issued, and that it allow Jews to immigrate at least to the extent permitted by immigration quotas, would likely have saved several hundred thousand people; but Roosevelt refused to do so. At times he even parroted Nazi anti-Jewish assertions.

For example, at the Casablanca conference in January 1943, while discussing possible projects for resettling rescued Jews in North Africa (projects subsequently

---

5   On Wallenberg, see ibid., 240–243; also, Arthur D. Morse, *While Six Million Died* (New York: Random House, 1967), 362–374.

6   Regarding the stance of major American Jewish organizations vis-à-vis immigration initiatives during this period, see in particular Medoff, *The Deafening Silence*.

torpedoed, mainly by the United States), Roosevelt suggested restricting the number of relocated Jews who were allowed to practice the professions, as this "would further eliminate the specific and understandable complaints which the Germans bore towards the Jews in Germany, namely that while they represented a small part of the population, over 50 percent of the lawyers, doctors, school teachers, college professors, etc. in Germany were Jews."[7] The figure for Jewish involvement in these occupations is, of course, wildly exaggerated. In addition, even if it were accurate, Roosevelt's assertion that it would render German animosity toward the Jews "understandable" hardly reflects well on him.

Caught up in rigid categorical thinking about who was with them and who was not, many Jews found it difficult to look objectively at Roosevelt. This was the leader who had forged the alliance of the underprivileged. Roosevelt's administration employed Jews at all levels in a manner that contrasted dramatically to the obstacles to employment Jews routinely encountered in the wider society. Essentially, Jews refused to acknowledge that he was not interested in offering succor to the Jews of Europe being murdered by the thousands daily in a program of total annihilation.

Rabbi Stephen Wise, leader of the American Jewish community and its efforts to promote rescue, defended Roosevelt even as he repeatedly encountered the administration's obstructionism. "[Roosevelt] is still our friend, even though he does not move as expeditiously as we would wish,"[8] he declared, and he took to task Jewish critics of the president. In June 1944, the Republican National Convention put a strong pro-Zionist plank in its platform for the upcoming election and criticized Roosevelt for not pressing Britain to open Mandate Palestine to Jewish refugees. In reaction, Wise wrote to Roosevelt, "As an American Jew and Zionist, I am deeply ashamed of the reference to you in the Palestine Resolution adopted by the Republican National Convention. It is utterly unjust, and you may be sure that American Jews will come to understand how unjust it is."[9]

This loyalty to Roosevelt also led the Jewish leadership to limit its work with the president's political foes in efforts to promote rescue. In contrast, the small group outside the leadership that did succeed in bringing about the creation of the War Refugee Board did not hesitate to work with sympathetic Republicans, which was a key factor in its success.

---

7   Cited in Deborah Lipstadt, *Beyond Belief* (New York: Free Press, 1986), 47–48.
8   Cited in Medoff, *The Deafening Silence*, 113.
9   Ibid., 178.

US Antisemitism Diminishes

In the decades after World War II, antisemitism in America dramatically diminished. Yet American Jews, according to polls, continued to believe otherwise. A 1990 survey of affiliated Jews showed that some seventy-five percent considered antisemitism a serious problem in the nation.[10] Perhaps for this reason, elements of the community continued to display psychological stigmata associated with besieged groups, such as the embracing of anti-Jewish canards.

American Jews have also believed antisemitism is more rife among American conservatives than liberals, even though, as noted earlier, actual surveys of American opinion regarding Jews do not support this assumption.[11] This is linked with the tendency to categorical thinking about political "allies," a wish to see protection as attainable by immersing Jewish interests in the interests of larger groups, particularly alliances of the disadvantaged, and a difficulty recognizing that perceived allies may not see things the way one imagines and wishes.

American Jews have, in fact, largely redefined the Jewish vocation, or Jewish identity, to focus mostly on alliances with, or in support of, the disadvantaged and the addressing of so-called "social justice" issues. Of course, pursuit of social justice has always been a central theme of Jewish religious teaching. And the reestablishment of the Jewish state was itself an act of social justice—a uniquely beleaguered and abused people exercising that right of self-determination extended to other peoples and establishing a base from which they can more readily cultivate their religiously mandated pursuit of charitable deeds and social justice in the wider world. But the current American Jewish focus on social justice very much reflects the cultivating of imagined transcendent alliances. It also reflects the pursuit of alliances with elite elements in the wider society, an exercise in ingratiation, as noted by Seymour Martin Lipset and Earl Raab: "[This emphasis] within the Jewish community [has] become most explicit when some of the main streams of American Christianity, usually the higher status denominations, have established a moralistic rather than a theological cast and espoused the 'social gospel.'"[12]

---

10 Lipset and Raab, *Jews and the New American Scene*, 69.
11 Ibid., 152.
12 Ibid., 54.

The 1960s and Beyond: A Mirror for the Present

In the post-World War II era, social liberalism became the common denominator of the greater part of the Jewish community. It is indicated, for example, by the results of a 1964 meeting of rabbis from the three major branches of Judaism who intended to try and reconcile their differences. The only common ground they could agree upon was support for the civil rights movement and the War on Poverty.[13] A 1988 survey conducted by the *Los Angeles Times* found that, when Jews were asked to consider pursuit of social justice and equality, support for Israel, and "religion" as three distinct facets of Jewish identity and to state which among them they most valued, many more chose the pursuit of social justice and equality (fifty percent) than either Israel (twenty percent) or religion (twenty percent).[14]

There is much to support the observation that alliances formed by the Jewish community around the promotion of social justice were motivated by more than simply the community's pragmatic self-interest in advancing social justice and equality. Nor was it merely a matter of the community's religious-ethical dedication to social justice as an abstract good. Rather, it reflected also the community's desire to demonstrate its benevolence, its transcending of parochialism, and its identification with larger groups, as a response to traditional anti-Jewish indictments. In particular, there is the evidence of major elements of the Jewish community being eager to embrace, cultivate, and cling to alliances with larger groups, and perceive an identity of interests in such alliances, even when the interests of the parties were clearly different and when aspects of the alliance were inimical to Jewish well-being. That eagerness has entailed an essentially delusional pursuit of an abstract concept of "proper Jewish behavior," born long ago in an atmosphere of Jews under siege; a pursuit largely maladaptive even then and no less maladaptive now.

For example, American Jews had always supported the movement first for Black emancipation and later for Black civil rights. Their doing so was obviously both morally correct and pragmatic. The National Jewish Community Relations Advisory Council (NJCRAC), renamed some years ago the Jewish Council for Public Affairs (JCPA)—an umbrella group of local Jewish Community Relations Councils across America—has always worked to

---

13   Jack Wertheimer, *A People Divided* (New York: Basic Books, 1993), 38.
14   Lipset and Raab, *Jews and the New American Scene*, 54 and 134.

promote Jewish-Black cooperation on social justice issues during its yearly conventions. However, Rabbi Arthur Hertzberg, himself a man of impeccable liberal credentials, notes that, while the organization's 1953 statement touches on what were indeed shared concerns and aims, it also suggests an identity of Black and Jewish interests that was not true. Hertzberg also points out that in the 1960s elements of the Black civil rights movement, and other groups that gained prominence within the American Black community, became radicalized, adopted a rhetoric that was often antisemitic, and pursued militant confrontations with the Jewish community:

> The richer and better established [segments of the Jewish community continued] to talk the older language of social conscience . . . The National Jewish Community Relations Advisory Council persisted in believing that the riots in the cities, in which Jewish stores in the black ghettos were main victims, were of little importance. In "program plan" after "program plan" the doctrine was reiterated that Jews should remain committed to every form of help for blacks. In late May 1967, the Anti-Defamation League published a study in five volumes on black anti-Semitism, to assert that there was less such prejudice among blacks than among whites. The Anti-Defamation League would soon change its estimate of black anti-Semitism, but in May 1967 this was the dominant "orthodoxy" of the American Jewish establishment.[15]

Jews have again and again embraced an uncritical, wishful, self-deluding comprehension of their interests being identical to all minorities' interests, or all interests couched in the rhetoric of supporting the disadvantaged. This idea was born largely of the anxieties and self-doubt engendered by being the targets of chronic marginalization and bias. But it has often left Jews unprepared for, and unresponsive to, anti-Jewish rhetoric and action emanating from their imagined soulmates.

In considering the American Jewish response to the increased antisemitism that characterized the domestic turmoil and political upheavals of the 1960s, we should also note the community's reaction to the recrudescence of populist antisemitism in the rhetoric of the so-called New Left. Couched in

---

15   Hertzberg, *The Jews in America*, 354.

a broader rhetoric of attacking institutional social injustice and championing a radically fairer and more equitable society, the new antisemitism elicited a generally weak response from Jewish communities and communal organizations. This remained so even after the 1967 war, when much of the New Left adopted a vehemently anti-Israel stance and ratcheted up its anti-Jewish rhetoric. Only the Jewish neoconservative movement, which developed largely in reaction to the New Left and represented a small minority of American Jews, addressed this 1960s incarnation of left-wing antisemitism directly and consistently.

Indeed, as in earlier decades in Europe, confronted with a rhetoric that characterized Jews as archetypal capitalists, exploiters of the downtrodden, a bulwark of the established system, and therefore an enemy that stood in the way of progress to a more equitable society, many Jews embraced the antisemitic indictment. Rather than attacking the bigots and the gross distortions of reality that they propagated, such people often urged Jewish self-reform consonant with the bigots' indictments. Rabbi Hertzberg notes that young Jews made up a significant part of the cadres of the New Left. He observes: "The adult Jewish supporters—or indulgers—of the New Left were not only some older radicals. The American Jewish establishment never really distanced itself from these young Jews."[16]

In subsequent decades, New Left perspectives became especially popular on university campuses. Today's widespread tolerance of campus antisemitism in America, amplified by other elements of the Red-Green-Black alliance, derives in no small part from those New Left roots. Jew-hatred in academia continues to be couched in the language of championing the disadvantaged. This rhetoric casts Jews as undeserving of protection under politically correct codes of conduct because of their supposed status as part of the dominant, white establishment. As noted in Chapter Three, the Jewish establishment's response to the ugly bigotry of the campuses, now as half a century ago, has fallen far short of the need.

The failure of the American Jewish community to respond in a meaningful way to the antisemitism coming in the 1960s from sources other than the Far Right concerns the Jew-hatred emanating from the Left and from Black radicals. Nothing has been said of the Palestinian/Islamist arm of the Red-Green-Black alliance and the Jew-hatred emanating from that source. But there were far fewer Palestinian/Islamist supporters in America half a century

16 Ibid., 357.

ago, and many less on the campuses, in the media, in local and state government, in the federal bureaucracy, and in Congress. So there was relatively little
domestic antisemitism from that quarter, and little for the Jewish community
to respond to, or fail to respond to, from that quarter.

But there was much antisemitism coming from the Arab states at that time.
In addition, there were incessant, intense attacks on Jews and the Jewish state,
largely instigated by Arab and other Muslim states, in the United Nations and
its agencies. Jewish organizations managed to generate some pushback in the
face of this onslaught. For example, as noted in Chapter Three, the "Mission
and History" section at the ADL's website references the organization's "1952
exposé, *The Troublemakers*, documenting how Arab propaganda in the U.S.
explicitly sought to foment anti-Israel and anti-Jewish sentiments." Also,
for the 1970s, the site notes efforts to counter the Arab boycott of Israel,
expose PLO and other Arab links to terrorism, and highlight the UN General
Assembly's hypocrisy in its dealings with Israel. Such efforts are evidence that
the ADL's attention to the problem of Arab antisemitism was greater at that
time than in more recent decades. Yet even then it fell short of the need.

The American Jewish Committee likewise sought in the latter decades
of the last century to call attention to antisemitism in the Arab and broader
Muslim world, as in its sponsorship of the excellent 2002 monograph by
Robert Wistrich, *Muslim Anti-Semitism: A Clear and Present Danger.*[17] Those
endeavors, too, seem more robust than those directed by the AJC at current
anti-Jewish bigotry emanating from the Arab and wider Muslim world. And
yet, even then they did not fully correspond to the need.

In recent years, particularly in the context of the Abraham Accords, there
has been some decrease in the promotion of antisemitism in several Arab
nations. But, more generally, Arab education systems, state-controlled media,
and religious institutions have long made anti-Jewish hatemongering standard
fare, including advancement of an explicitly genocidal agenda. In the wake of
the Arab defeat in the 1967 Six-Day War, exporting of that antisemitism—via
Arab initiatives at the United Nations and other international forums, via
Arab infiltration of foreign education systems, and via the efforts of overseas
arms of Arab media—became a major tool of a global information war targeting Israel and Jews. Within the Arab states, beyond the pervasive drumbeat
of Jew-hatred coming from the schools, media, and mosques, *Mein Kampf*

---

17   Robert Wistrich, *Muslim Anti-Semitism: A Clear and Present Danger* (New York: American
      Jewish Committee, 2002).

and *The Protocols of the Elders of Zion* have been widely translated, published, and distributed, often with government subsidy.[18] Holocaust denial has been commonplace, along with the logically inconsistent, but programmatically related, praising of Hitler for his extermination of Europe's Jews. Blood libels have likewise been commonplace, with Jews accused of using Muslim blood to make holiday pastries or for other ritual purposes. Jews have been characterized as satanic or subhuman and their murder labeled the will of God and a religious duty.

Bernard Lewis, perhaps the West's premier authority in Middle Eastern studies, wrote in 1986 regarding antisemitism in the Arab world:

> The volume of anti-Semitic books and articles published, the size and number of editions and impressions, the eminence and authority of those who write, publish, and sponsor them, their place in school and college curricula, their role in the mass media, would all seem to suggest that classical anti-Semitism is an essential part of Arab intellectual life at the present time—almost as much as happened in Nazi Germany, and considerably more than in late nineteenth- and early twentieth-century France.[19]

As noted, some American Jewish organizations have at times condemned the endemic antisemitism in much of the Muslim world and the role of Muslim governments in promoting it. But, in general, the communal response to this "Third World" antisemitism, and to its embrace by the Arabs' and Muslims' leftist sympathizers in Europe and America, has been remarkably different from the reaction to European and American manifestations of right-wing antisemitism. American Jewish groups have routinely responded much more energetically and emphatically to the threats from the Western Right. Of course, these threats are no less vile, but by all measures they have received much less popular support and been much less of an immediate danger in the last half-century.

---

18 See, for example, "Anti-Semitism Goes Viral at the Cairo Book Fair," Simon Wiesenthal Center, February 6, 2023. Also, Andrew Weinberg, "ADL Study Finds Ongoing Use of Anti-Semitic Materials at State-Run Book Fairs across Arab World," ADL, February 25, 2020, https://www.adl.org/resources/article/adl-study-finds-ongoing-use-anti-semitic-materials-state-run-book-fairs-across.
19 Bernard Lewis, *Semites and Anti-Semites* (New York: W. W. Norton, 1986), 357.

In October 1999, Joerg Haider, leader of a Far Right party in Austria, did unexpectedly well in national elections, and four months later Austria's president agreed to include Haider's party in a new coalition government. The outcry from American groups regarding these developments—understandable given Austria's history—was loud and sharp. But Haider's appointment represented a much lesser danger than the antisemitic invective being spewed at the very same time by the Syrian government, then as now officially at war with Israel. During these same months, Syria's state-controlled media ran several stories with antisemitic themes. One of them, published in late November 1999, regurgitated the blood libel, the claim that Jews use the blood of gentiles for their religious rituals, which was also the theme of a popular book by Syria's defense minister, Mustafa Tlas (*The Matzah of Zion*). An editorial in late January 2000, in Syria's leading newspaper, *Tishreen*, a mouthpiece for the Assad regime, focused on denial of the Holocaust while insisting that Israeli policies are worse than those of the Nazis. Yet these events in Syria received very little attention and condemnation from American Jewish groups.

The hostility of the United Nations to Jews and the Jewish state evolved—again largely in the wake of the 1967 war—as a joint effort of the Arab and larger Muslim bloc in the UN acting in concert with the Soviet bloc and with the general acquiescence of Western European states. The United Nations, in its formal mandate, obviously offers much that makes it an attractive institution to Jews simply from a pragmatic perspective, and even more to recommend it from the perspective of the Jewish embrace of international humanitarian causes. That mandate includes working against racism, bigotry, the abuse of populations due to prejudice, and, more broadly, against violence and for the peaceful resolution of conflicts. The United Nations' special agencies are charged with promoting world health, advancing education worldwide, and fighting the ravages of poverty, natural disasters, and war. It is hardly surprising the American Jews and their communal organizations have been broadly supportive of the United Nations since its inception. What is noteworthy in the present context is how slow much of the Jewish community has been to change its position and challenge the United Nations and various of its constituent bodies even as they have for decades promulgated blatant hostility to Israel and indeed to Jews generally.

Every year, no matter what acts of war, enslavement, and even genocide are unfolding elsewhere in the world, more General Assembly resolutions are devoted to attacks on Israel than to any other subject.[20] In 1975, the Assembly, at the instigation of the Soviet Union, its satellites, and the Arab states, passed a scurrilous resolution equating Zionism with racism. Its chief proponents were states that routinely practiced the most horrendous abuses of their ethnic and religious minorities. The General Assembly only repealed the resolution, under intense American pressure, in 1991.

The UN's special agencies like UNESCO and WHO have been subverted to anti-Israel agendas; conferences on women's rights or vital medical issues have routinely become forums dedicated to Arab attacks on Israel. The UN Commission for Human Rights and its successor body, the UN Human Rights Council, have been particularly ugly in their indicting and defaming Israel, exemplified by the commission's choreographing an orgy of Jew-hatred at the August 2001 Durban conference on racism and other forms of bigotry. An April 2002 vote by the commission's member states endorsed terrorist attacks against Israeli civilians.[21]

The United Nations early and eagerly embraced the Palestine Liberation Organization (PLO) even though the PLO charter calls for the annihilation of a UN member state. The UN Relief and Works Agency for Palestinian Refugees (UNRWA), whose responsibilities over more than seven decades have included educating young Palestinians in schools in UN-administered refugee camps, routinely taught the antisemitism that was a staple of the Arab school texts used in the West Bank and Gaza before 1967. After the 1967 war, Israel expunged anti-Israel and anti-Jewish material from textbooks in the territories but not from the books used in UNRWA schools, which continued with their hate-filled "education."

Since the establishment of the Palestinian Authority (PA) in 1994, UNRWA has been providing its students with PA textbooks, teaching that Jews are evil, that they have no legitimate presence in the land of Israel and are merely usurpers, and that it is not only the right but the duty of Palestinian children to pursue Israel's annihilation.[22] The stipulations of

20 On the UN General Assembly and Israel, see, for example, Allison Kaplan Sommer, "The UN's Outcast: Why is Israel Treated Differently Than All Other Nations?" Reform Judaism Online, Winter 2002.
21 See, for example, Steven Edwards, "UN Backs Palestinian Violence: Arab, European Nations Pass Resolution Supporting Use of 'Armed Struggle,'" National Post (Canada), April 16, 2002, A1.
22 On UNRWA-administered schools, see, for example, Matthew Kalman, "Canadian Funds Help Promote Hatred: Palestinian Schools Teach Glory of Martyrs, Deny Israel's Existence," The Ottawa Citizen, November 24, 2001; Charles A. Radin, "UN Role in

the Oslo accords calling for an end to incitement had no more impact on UNRWA's policies than on the Palestinian Authority. When questioned about the hatemongering and incitement to anti-Israel and anti-Jewish violence in UNRWA school texts, UNRWA commissioner-general at the time, Peter Hansen, responded, "We cannot expect a people under occupation fighting every day to have textbooks which idealize, praise and express love for their occupiers."[23]

UNRWA has allowed its facilities to be used as recruiting and training grounds and armories for terrorists, providing an important strategic resource for terrorist groups targeting Israeli civilians.[24] Hamas's seizure of Gaza from the PA in 2007 (Israel had withdrawn from Gaza in 2005) had no impact on this pattern, and UNRWA's facilitating of Hamas terrorism emanating from Gaza has continued to the present. Indeed, significant numbers of UNRWA teachers and other employees in Gaza have been affiliated with Hamas.

All UNRWA's denials of the indoctrination of its students in genocidal Jew-hatred and the involvement of its teachers and its other staff with Hamas should have been dispelled by the events of October 7, 2023, and the evidence of such involvement subsequently uncovered by Israel, including the participation of some UNRWA employees in the massacre. The celebration of the October 7 atrocities by hundreds of UNRWA staff on social media provided further evidence of UNRWA's intimate connections with Hamas and its war crimes. Yet the disingenuous and hypocritical denials of those connections, seconded by other UN institutions, persist.

Through all this, while some American Jewish organizations have at times challenged the nefarious role of the United Nations, no concerted effort has been made by American Jewish leadership, or demanded by its constituents, to call out the scope and breadth of the UN's role in promoting and advancing policies aimed at isolating and ultimately annihilating Israel. This failure seems to be at least in part because the UN's official objectives render it the kind of organization that Jews, whose self-identity is centered on social liberalism and universalism, are supposed to support.

Palestinian Camps in Dispute: Critics Say Extremism Appeased," *The Boston Globe*, July 8, 2002; Michael Wines, "Killing of UN Aide by Israel Bares Rift with Relief Agency," *New York Times*, January 4, 2003.

23   Cited in "UNRWA Seeks to Calm Row over Palestinian Textbooks," *Jordan Times*, August 30, 2001.

24   See, for example, Herb Keinon, "Shin Bet Documents Terrorists' Misuse of UNRWA Facilities," *Jerusalem Post*, December 11, 2002.

American Jewish Predilections and Politics

American Jewish political patterns took much of their present form during the Roosevelt administration. They changed little through the 1960s and beyond. The New Left, while establishing a significant foothold in the 1960s in academia and in other bastions of the Left, did not have a very marked impact on the policies of the Democrat Party. Likewise, the Black radicalism of the era and the antisemitism emanating from the Arab world had relatively little impact on Democrat policies on a national scale. There was, in essence, little coming from the party during this time that challenged the political predilections of American Jews. This was largely true as well across subsequent decades.

But, in the last approximately fifteen years, the situation has changed. The presidency of Barack Obama raised various red flags for American Jews. His promotion of the Muslim Brotherhood in Egypt, apart from destabilizing that nation, also entailed dangers for Israel. Throughout his time in office, Obama was notably cool to the Jewish state. His courting of Iran, culminating in the nuclear deal that provided the Iranian regime with an internationally endorsed pathway to nuclear weapons—even as Iran was consistently reiterating its commitment to Israel's annihilation—obviously presented a more direct, existential threat to Israel. So, too, did Obama's subsidies to the Iranian mullahs of more than a hundred billion dollars with which to pursue their terror campaigns throughout the Middle East and beyond.

Obama's explicit disavowing of prior American assurances to Israel regarding its presence in parts of the West Bank, particularly those made in the context of Israel's withdrawal from Gaza and some West Bank areas, had additional negative impact on the Jewish state. So did related moves by Obama; most notably his choreographing, in a dramatic departure from all previous presidents, a Security Council resolution demanding Israel's withdrawal to the pre-1967 armistice lines—which would render the nation indefensible.

While the deleterious consequences of Obama's policies fell primarily on Israel and not American Jews, it would be wrong to believe that the latter were not directly hurt by those policies as well. The largesse provided by Obama to the Iranian regime helped finance its elaborately funded and widely publicized campaigns of Holocaust denial. Choreographed in collaboration with prominent antisemites from Western and other nations, these campaigns helped legitimize Iran's big lie across much of the globe. They were directed at discrediting and demonizing all Jews, not just Israelis. More substantively,

Iran used the Obama-provided windfall to finance its terrorist allies including Hezbollah in Lebanon and Hamas in Gaza. Hamas, as noted, has declared as its objective and religious obligation the murder of all the world's Jews, not just Israelis. And the leader of Hezbollah stated that he prefers to see the world's Jews immigrate to Israel as that will save his organization the trouble of having to track them down across the globe. In fact, of course, Hezbollah and Iran have acted on their genocidal antisemitism all over the world. For example, they blew up the Israeli embassy in Buenos Aires in 1992, killing twenty-nine people, including Argentine Jews and non-Jews, and two years later they murdered eighty-five people by bombing the city's Jewish culture center, specifically targeting Argentine Jews (and again killing a number of non-Jews as well). American Jews are not exempt from similar treatment by the mullahs and their allies, and Obama's pro-Iranian policies and generosity to the theocrats in Tehran greatly increased their capacity for such violence.

In domestic policies as well, Obama compromised the well-being of American Jews. Perhaps most notably, his sowing of racial divisiveness, a challenge to all Americans, represented a particular threat to Jews. Jews are the minority most associated with promotion of the integrationist agenda advanced by Martin Luther King, Jr., and his allies in the civil rights movement of the mid-twentieth century. Obama's cultivating of a racial divide inspired increased numbers, Black and White, to reject the integrationist ideal. Consequently, many people started looking negatively at the Jews because they were so closely identified with that ideal.

Yet Obama's actions had little substantive impact on the pro-Democrat policy preferences and voting patterns of American Jews. In the years since Obama's two terms in office, the Democrats' so-called progressive wing, with its Far Left leanings and its promotion of a still more aggressive racial divisiveness, has gained an ever greater influence over party policy. Its championing—as noted in Chapter One—of "critical race theory" and of the agenda characterized as advancing "diversity, equity, and inclusion," are marked by widespread targeting of Jews as white, unfairly successful, and, again, too pro-integration. Jews are too much in favor of judging people as individuals rather than as avatars of a group identity; too concerned with the content of a person's character and not enough with the color of his or her skin or with other racial or ethnic identifiers. Yet most Jews have remained loyal to the party.

Other efforts of the various arms of the Red-Green-Black alliance to mainstream Jew-hatred in America have also been abetted by the Democrat Party.

For example, when Representative Ilhan Omar shared anti-Jewish tropes and memes not long after her initial election to Congress in 2018, the Democrat Party could not bring itself to pass a straightforward condemnation of her antisemitism. Instead, it acceded to Democrat caucus pressure and issued a bland generic critique of all bigotries. Omar and fellow representative Rashida Tlaib, likewise given to anti-Jewish rhetoric, refused to join a party-sponsored trip to Israel for new members of Congress in the summer of 2019. They insisted on having their travels sponsored by a Palestinian organization, Miftah, notorious for its Holocaust denial, its accusations that Jews use the blood of Christians to prepare Passover matzah, and its promotion of anti-Jewish terror. The Democrat Party leadership's response was not to criticize the two Congresswomen, but to attack Israel for preventing their entry for the Miftah tour. In the 2020 Democratic primaries, both Omar and Tlaib faced Democrat challengers less hostile to Jews. Yet House Speaker Pelosi endorsed the bigoted incumbents to be the party's nominees.

In the wake of October 7, 2023, when Hamas slaughtered over 1,200 Israelis and kidnapped some 240 others, President Biden came out strongly in support of Israel's determination to dismantle Hamas and end its control of Gaza. But he faced significant pushback from fellow Democrats who, together with a bloc of the party's Congressional delegation, defended Hamas and demanded Biden withdraw his backing of the Israeli response to the slaughter. When Representative Tlaib reacted to the Hamas assault and the Israeli initiation of anti-Hamas hostilities by calling for the destruction of Israel and the creation of a Palestinian state "from the river to the sea," the House of Representatives passed a motion to censure her by a vote of 234 to 188. But only twenty-two Democrats out of a delegation of 184 voted for the motion.

The Democrat Party has embraced the Black Lives Matter movement. It has ignored the anti-Jewish rhetoric of BLM leaders, and was silent as BLM mobs attacked and defaced synagogues and targeted Jewish-owned properties in, for example, the Fairfax section of Los Angeles.

At the Democrat convention in August 2020, places of honor were accorded to acolytes of Nation of Islam's Louis Farrakhan, such as Jew-bashers Linda Sarsour and Tamika Mallory, as well as Farrakhan promoter Pastor Frederick Haynes, who was featured at the convention's "Our Values" Black Caucus event. Imam Noman Hussain, notorious for inciting hatred of non-believers, particularly Jews, was given a place of honor at the convention's "Interfaith Welcome Service." After some criticism of Sarsour's role at the convention—and noting of its inconsistency with the Biden campaign's efforts to project an image of moderation—the Biden camp issued a statement criticizing Sarsour. That criticism unleashed a backlash by many in the party, and the administration subsequently issued an unpublicized apology.

The Democrat Party has also been essentially silent about growing hostility towards Jews promoted in Democrat bastions in the wider society. The major American institutions abetting antisemitism are, again, its colleges and universities, dominated by Democrats. The party has made no effort to curb this disgrace.

In response to the post-October 7 explosion of antisemitism on college and university campuses across the nation, the Republican-controlled House of Representatives held hearings on institutional failures to address the rampant Jew-hatred. After Republican senators called for similar hearings in the Senate in March 2024, the Democrat Senate leadership delayed the hearings until the following fall and then diverted attention from the onslaught against Jews by shifting the subject to hatreds more generally.[25] (The spillover from the campuses that saw leftist and Islamist-led anti-Israel and anti-Jewish demonstrations, often accompanied by violence, in the streets of cities across the nation, were actually cheered on by some Democrats, including Vice President Harris.)[26] This Jew-hatred is rapidly expanding from higher education into public and private schools, often aided by Democrat state and local governments, and there, too, it proceeds unchecked by the party.

All of this has still had relatively little impact on American Jewish political affiliations and voting practices. The American Jewish Committee's "annual survey of American Jewish opinion," released shortly before Barack Obama's first election to the White House and reflecting polling from September 8 to September 21, 2008, reported that 56% of American Jews identified themselves as Democrats, 17% as Republicans (and 25% as Independents).[27] The AJC survey of 2021 showed that 51% of American Jews described themselves as Democrats, 13% as Republicans (and 22% as Independents, while the remaining 14% characterized themselves as embracing some Other affiliation or as not knowing). In the election of 2008, exit polls suggested that about

---

25 See, for example, "Graham Condemns Rise in Anti-Semitism at Senate Judiciary Committee Hearing," U.S. Senate Committee on the Judiciary, September 19, 2024, https://www.judiciary.senate.gov/press/rep/releases/graham-condemns-rise-in-anti-semitism-at-senate-judiciary-committee-hearing.

26 See, for example, Philip Klein, "Kamala Harris Says Anti-Israel Student Protestors 'are showing exactly what the human emotion should be,'" National Review, July 8, 2024.

27 "2008 Annual Survey of American Jewish Opinion," American Jewish Committee, September 2008.

three-quarters of American Jews voted for Obama.[28] While exit polls are often unreliable, a Gallup poll conducted shortly before the election yielded similar numbers, with Obama leading John McCain among Jews by 74% to 22%.[29] An Associated Press survey of polls on the election pattern in 2020 indicated that it is likely Biden got about 70% of the Jewish vote and Trump about 30%.[30]

Exit polls for the 2024 presidential election indicated that in many sections of the nation, including heavily Jewish precincts in New York, New Jersey, California, Florida, Pennsylvania, and Michigan, Donald Trump did substantially better among Jews than previously, and better than other Republican presidential candidates in recent decades.[31] In other areas, however, Trump's numbers seem to have been closer to those garnered by him and by other Republicans in prior elections, with little indication that Democrat Party proclivities inimical to Jews have had a major impact on Jewish loyalty to the party.

No doubt, a number of American Jews, confronted with the dissonance between their traditional embrace of left-of-center political views and allegiance to the Democrat Party, on the one hand, and concern over the party's increasing anti-Jewish predilections on the other, have been moved to a reassessment of their party loyalty. But many are those who, in the face of collective memories of anti-Jewish depredations, have hollowed out their "Jewish" identity and reduced it primarily to a political commitment to the Left imagined as a protective alliance of the traditionally targeted and disadvantaged, or at least have given to such a political commitment priority in their comprehension of themselves as Jews. Such individuals are likely to remain willfully blind to the incompatibility between American Jewish well-being and loyalty to a political party that has demonstrated a willingness to sacrifice that well-being to please other constituencies. They will buttress that blindness with rationalizations such as noting that many leading Democrats still seem genuinely concerned with the welfare of the Jewish community,

28 See, for example, Hilary Leila Krieger, "Exit Polls: 78% of Jews Voted for Obama," *Jerusalem Post*, November 5, 2008.
29 Lydia Saad, "Obama Winning Over the Jewish Vote," Gallup Poll News Service, October 23, 2008.
30 See, for example, Gabriel Greschler, "Trump or Biden—How did Jewish Voters Line Up This Year? It's Complicated," Jewish News of Northern California, November 6, 2020.
31 See, for example, Armin Rosen, "Who Won the Jewish Vote?" *Tablet Magazine*, November 14, 2024.

and that, if the party gives priority to other considerations inconsistent with the well-being of Jews, its doing so can be construed as helping some disadvantaged groups and so converges with the Jewish mission of *tikkun olam* ("healing the world"). They may even urge Jewish communal self-reform to appease the anti-Jewish indictments coming from the progressive wing of the Democrat Party and from its partners in the Red-Green-Black alliance.

Such willful blindness and buttressing rationalizations will also be embraced by those Jews whose self-comprehension entails identification with Democrat-leaning elements of the wider society that have embraced anti-Jewish positions, such as academia, much of the media and cultural elites, the "liberal" churches, and others. They will, in effect, prioritize loyalty to those elements over Jewish well-being.

It is unclear whether or not the increasing antisemitism in America will reach a point where even those who have so far been loath to rethink their political loyalties will be swayed to challenge the threats to the American Jewish community, or—if they do so—will act in time to defang the threats. But the answer to that question will go far in determining the fate of Jewish well-being in America.

Chapter Six

American Jews and Israel[1]

_____

"We consider ourselves no longer a nation, but a religious community, and therefore expect neither a return to Palestine, nor a sacrificial worship under the sons of Aaron, nor the restoration of any of the laws concerning the Jewish state."

Reform Judaism's "Pittsburgh Platform," 1885

"The death of Tony Judt, historian of contemporary Europe, offers an opportunity to revisit a case of strongly anti-Zionist sentiments held by a prominent Jewish intellectual . . . [I]t was the New York University lecturer's polemical essays and public statements against Zionism, and his rejection of the legitimacy of the Jewishness of the State of Israel, that thrust him onto the public stage. In a much-cited October 2003 essay in _The New York Review of Books_, Judt called to dismantle the state and to replace it with 'a single, integrated, bi-national state' between the Jordan River and the Mediterranean Sea—a recipe for national suicide for the sovereign Jewish entity . . . 'The behavior of a self-described Jewish state affects the way everyone else looks at Jews,' wrote Judt. His solution? Do away with [Israel]."

Jerusalem Post editorial, August 8, 2010

In his groundbreaking Zionist _cri de coeur_, _The Jewish State_, Theodor Herzl acknowledged that his proposal for officially establishing a Jewish homeland would inevitably face numerous objections. He observed, "Perhaps we

---

1   A version of this chapter was previously published, under the title "American Jews and Their Israel Problem," as Mideast Security and Policy Studies No. 159, The Begin-Sadat Center for Strategic Studies, Bar-Ilan University, Ramat Gan, Israel, December 31, 2018.

shall have to fight first of all against many an evil-disposed, narrow-hearted, short-sighted member of our own race."[2] In fact, Jewish antizionism preceded Herzl's book by many decades.

As previously noted, the issue of extending civic rights to Jews was first broached in Central European polities in the late eighteenth and early nineteenth centuries, and those opposed to granting such rights cited supposed characteristics of "the Jews" that, to their view, rendered them unfit. One of those disqualifying characteristics was that Jews were a separate nation. As with the other assertions mustered against them, some Jews took the indictment to heart and strove to reform themselves to counter it. They sought to win over those purveying or subscribing to the "Jews as a nation" indictment by demonstrating that they had abandoned the accoutrements of national identity and had transformed themselves into a purely religious community. For example, Jews so disposed established new, reformist congregations in German states, congregations in which the liturgy was stripped of all references to longing for Jerusalem and Zion and all aspirations for national rebirth.

Moreover, as with Jewish accommodation of other anti-Jewish arguments, those Jews who took this step often sought to cast their doing so not as an attempt to appease their attackers but rather as a high-minded ethical decision. They argued that over the preceding two millennia Judaism had evolved from its dual, national and universal, identity into an embrace of a universal moral and ethical belief system and mission. Any persistence or recrudescence of national identity and aspirations was, they insisted, atavistic and had to be shunned by modern, enlightened Jews.

Reformist German Jews brought their antizionist predilections with them to the United States. As the Reform movement organized itself in America, it repeatedly reiterated these sentiments. For example, the Reform "Pittsburgh Platform" of 1885 declared, "We consider ourselves no longer a nation, but a religious community, and therefore expect neither a return to Palestine, nor a sacrificial worship under the sons of Aaron, nor the restoration of any of the laws concerning the Jewish state."[3]

With Zionism gaining greater traction among many Jews at the beginning of the last century, Jewish antizionism also grew, spurred in large part by fears that Jewish civic advancement, the accommodation of Jews as equal citizens

---

2   Theodor Herzl, *The Jewish State* (New York: Dover, 1988), 154.

3   "Reform Judaism: The Pittsburgh Platform (November 1885)," Jewish Virtual Library, https://www.jewishvirtuallibrary.org/the-pittsburgh-platform.

in parts of Europe and in the United States, would be undercut by the creation of a Jewish state. For example, much of the domestic opposition to Britain's issuing of the Balfour Declaration in 1917 arose from elements of British Jewry moved by such concerns.

In the United States, Louis Brandeis was very much an exception within the Jewish establishment when he enthusiastically embraced Zionism and dismissed concerns that the wider community's support for a Jewish state would undercut Jews' standing in America. Speaking in 1915, Brandeis noted the demands for self-determination by Europe's minorities that had preceded the war then raging in Europe and would have to be addressed in its aftermath. He noted as well America's sympathy with these minorities and construed Zionism as consistent with these other peoples' aspirations and with the supportive American perspective.[4] Elsewhere the same year, Brandeis posed the question, "While every other people is striving for development by asserting its nationality, and a great war is making clear the value of small nations, shall we [Jews] voluntarily yield to anti-Semitism [that is, to fears of an antisemitic backlash], and instead of solving our 'problem' end it by noble suicide?"[5]

But, again, Brandeis was an exception within elite Jewish circles in America. More representative were those who feared that Zionism would undermine the Jews' civic gains. *New York Times* publisher Adolph Ochs insisted that Jews must eschew ethnic or "national" group identity. He wrote, "I'm interested in the Jewish religion—I want to see it preserved—but that's as far as I want to go." Ochs castigated Brandeis for having become, with his embrace of Zionism, "a professional Jew."[6]

Brandeis's wartime predictions proved prescient. After the war, a number of new nation states were established in Eastern Europe out of territories of the former German, Austro-Hungarian, and Russian empires. In addition, Syrian and Iraqi mandates for the creation of Arab states and the Palestine mandate for the establishment of a Jewish national home were carved out of lands previously part of the Ottoman Empire.

The World War I allies' endorsement of the Zionist project, as well as its subsequent approval by the League of Nations, drew some Jews out of the antizionist camp in the United States. In addition, in the post-war decades, a

---

4   Louis Brandeis, *Brandeis on Zionism: A Collection of Addresses and Statements by Louis D. Brandeis* (Washington, D.C.: Zionist Organization of America, 1942), 11.

5   Ibid., 23.

6   Gay Talese, *The Kingdom and the Power* (New York: World, 1966), 168.

number of Reform rabbis with pro-Zionist views, such as Abba Hillel Silver, Stephen S. Wise, and Nelson Glueck, rose to prominence within both Reform and Zionist circles. The straitened, continually worsening circumstances of Jewish communities in Central and Eastern Europe in the decades between the world wars also had some impact on attitudes towards Zionism. But while Reform Judaism's Columbus Platform of 1937 reflects some of these influences and associated changes, it also conveys what had not changed:

> In all lands where our people live, they assume and seek to share loyally the full duties and responsibilities of citizenship and to create seats of Jewish knowledge and religion. In the rehabilitation of Palestine, the land hallowed by memories and hopes, we behold the promise of renewed life for many of our brethren. We affirm the obligation of all Jewry to aid in its upbuilding as a Jewish homeland by endeavoring to make it not only a haven of refuge for the oppressed but also a center of Jewish culture and spiritual life.[7]

This statement starts by seeking to counter the "dual loyalty" canard, which many feared was the inevitable outcome of the Zionist project. It then acknowledges the potential role of the new homeland as a haven, "the promise of a new life," for Jews increasingly under siege in Eastern and Central Europe. It concludes by seeking to accommodate both the need and the fear: Jews are enjoined to help in the building of the homeland/refuge, but it is envisioned not as an independent Jewish state—an entity that might, again, provide hostile forces with ammunition for claims of divided loyalty and grounds for curbing Jews' civic gains—but rather as a "center of Jewish culture and spiritual life."

This distinction, with its anti-state bias, had significant consequences. Its translation into concrete action by Felix Warburg and Rabbi Judah Magnes, chronicled by Yoram Hazony in The Jewish State, is illustrative.[8] Warburg, a leading figure in the German Jewish elite in America, had earlier agreed to be a major donor to Hebrew University in Jerusalem, founded in 1919. While in

---

7   "Reform Judaism: The Columbus Platform (1937)," Jewish Virtual Library, https://www. jewishvirtuallibrary.org/the-columbus-platform-1937.

8   Yoram Hazony, The Jewish State: The Struggle for Israel's Soul (New York: Basic Books, 2000).

favor of building a cultural and religious center in the Mandate such as alluded to in the Columbus Platform, he was an opponent of Zionist aspirations to a state. He conditioned his support of the university on the appointment of American Reform Rabbi Judah Magnes, who shared Warburg's views on the proper objective of the Zionist project, to a dominant position in the university, ultimately to the post of university chancellor, and to control of the funds. (At the time of his Hebrew University appointment, Magnes was associate rabbi at Temple Beth El in Manhattan.)

In the ensuing years, both Warburg and Magnes fought aggressively against the pursuit of a Jewish state. Both, for example, perceived the 1929 Arab assault on, and massacre of, Jews in the Mandate, including the murder of sixty-seven Jews in Hebron, as an opportunity to undermine the Jewish quest for a state by presenting it as the source of Arab enmity. In October 1929, Magnes met with a confidant of the grand mufti, Haj Amin al-Husseini, who had instigated the massacre. Together with the mufti's representative, he formulated a proposal for the establishment of an Arab-controlled government in the Mandate and the abandonment of Jewish aspirations to a state.[9]

When the leadership of the Yishuv, the Jewish community in the Mandate, rejected the plan, Warburg threatened that American Jewish support would be cut off if the Magnes initiative was not embraced. Nevertheless, both the elected Assembly of the Yishuv and the Zionist Executive refused to endorse it.

Magnes's meeting with a member of the Mufti's camp had been arranged by *New York Times* correspondent and avowed antizionist Joseph Levi. After the rejection of his initiative, Magnes embarked on a publicity campaign to promote his views and attack the pro-state Zionists. The *New York Times*, under the aegis of the no less antizionist Adolph Ochs, gave prominent coverage and editorial support to Magnes's stance.[10]

In the spring of 1936, the Grand Mufti again launched attacks against the Jews of the Yishuv, this time in a sustained onslaught that also included attacks against British forces. The following year, the British appointed the Peel Commission to investigate the unrest and formulate recommendations in response to the violence. The commission proposed partition of the

---

9   Ibid., 213–214. Magnes's interlocutor was Harry St. John Philby.

10   Ibid., 215. See also Arthur A. Goren, ed., *Dissenter in Zion: From the Writings of Judah L. Magnes* (Cambridge, MA: Harvard University Press, 1982), document 66, "An International Enclave," 282–285. The document was published in the *New York Times*, November 24, 1929.

Mandate into independent Jewish and Arab states. The Jewish state would consist of about four percent of the original Palestine Mandate. The League of Nations objected to the proposal, insisting that it violated Britain's obligations to the Jews under the Mandate. However, the Yishuv leadership, led by David Ben-Gurion, agreed to the recommendation, prompted by recognition of the looming catastrophe in Europe and understanding that even this mini-state would offer European Jews a refuge. Ben-Gurion argued, "Through which [option] can we get in the shortest possible time the most Jews in Palestine? . . . How much greater will be the absorptive capacity without an alien, unconcerned . . . hostile administration, but with a Zionist government . . . holding the key to immigration in its hand."[11]

Warburg, in contrast, vehemently denounced the partition plan, arguing that acceptance of the Peel proposal reflected a Zionist "lust for power" and "a concept of Jewish life which is abhorrent."[12] This hyperbolic vilification, and the cold indifference to the desperate plight of Europe's Jews, seem incomprehensible unless recognized as representing, beneath the claims of high-mindedness and moral integrity, a response to anti-Jewish pressures and, more particularly, fears that creation of a Jewish state would compromise the fragile status of Jews in America and elsewhere in the West.

The Peel Commission recommendations were rejected by the Arabs and withdrawn by Britain. The British subsequently issued the infamous White Paper, which dramatically limited Jewish immigration, proposed the ultimate establishment of an Arab-dominated government in the Mandate, and essentially cut off the one internationally recognized refuge for a doomed European Jewry.

Magnes continued his own attacks on those favoring the establishment of a Jewish state even after revelation of the genocide unfolding in Europe. In 1943, he wrote articles on the topic for American as well as British publications. Perhaps his most consistent outlet was the *New York Times*, where publisher Arthur Hay Sulzberger (who had succeeded Adolph Ochs in 1935) had instructed that editorial policy on the Mandate "be predicated on the Magnes point of view."[13] Indeed, that view was promoted in *New York Times'* editorials and news stories. Magnes pursued his campaign after the war as

---

11   Cited in Shabtai Teveth, *Ben-Gurion: The Burning Ground* (Boston, MA: Houghton, Mifflin, 1987), 611–612.
12   Cited in Hazony, *The Jewish State*, 231.
13   Ibid., 247.

well, even coming to the States at the urging of the State Department to lobby against the United Nations partition plan.[14]

But the genocide in Europe, and Britain's policy throughout the war of blocking Jewish access to the Mandate and obstructing rescue, significantly eroded the ranks of the anti-state camp within the American Jewish elite. Further defections followed during Israel's war of independence against surrounding countries that had publicly declared their intention to annihilate the Yishuv and its population, and then with the actual establishment of the state.

One notable indication of the shift within American Reform Judaism's leadership regarding the Zionist project is that the pro-Zionist rabbi and archaeologist Nelson Glueck became head of Hebrew Union College (HUC), the premier Reform seminary. Under Glueck's leadership, the HUC ultimately established a campus in Jerusalem, where all first-year HUC students were to study.

Beyond the shift in the leadership, Reform congregants—by far the largest body of synagogue-affiliated Jews in America—overwhelmingly became supporters of Israel. That bond increased even further with the threats to Israel in the lead-up to and during the 1967 war.

And Yet . . .

What, then, accounts for the fact that some within the leadership of Reform Judaism, including within the rabbinate, and a significant proportion of Reform congregants, seem to have discarded their identification with Israel in recent decades? While this disconnection among Reform Jews is less than among religiously unaffiliated Jews, it is still substantive. This shift is commonly attributed to generational differences, as people who have now come of age are far removed from the Shoah, Israel's creation, and the Six-Day War. But there are more specific factors at work as well.

The key factor driving Reform antizionism into the middle of the twentieth century was the then century-old anti-Jewish indictment that Jewish nationhood disqualified Jews from being given full civic rights in European states. This, and subsequent fears that any civic rights achieved would be rolled back in response to the Zionist movement, drove many Jews to argue that they were no longer a nation but exclusively a religious community.

---

14   See Goren, *Dissenter in Zion*, 461–520.

The open identification of most Reform Jews with Israel in the decades after the state's establishment was made much easier by the fact that the Jewish state was viewed favorably by large swathes of non-Jewish Americans. But there are many Jews who, whether by virtue of profession or other elements of self-identity, draw their sense of themselves from affiliations with cadres on the American scene that are less sympathetic to Israel, such as academia, the left-leaning media, the so-called "liberal" Protestant churches, or particular political groups. Such Jews have typically been less committed to Israel. As those non-Jewish cadres have in recent years exhibited broader and more intense hostility to Israel, Jews who identify with them—whether Reform, of some other denomination, or unaffiliated—have become even more inclined to distance themselves from Israel.

Another anti-Jewish indictment, related to but distinct from the "Jews as a nation" critique, is the accusation that Jews are too parochial in their interests, are concerned only with their own, and are therefore not fit to be accepted fully as part of the larger political body. This accusation can also be traced, in its political impact, to early nineteenth-century Europe, and it continues to shape Jewish politics in America. For two hundred years, many Jewish groups have responded to the indictment by laboring to demonstrate their commitment to causes beyond the Jewish community, doing so even when those causes have run counter to Jewish interests.

Perhaps no institutions in American Jewish life more dramatically reflect this phenomenon than Jewish Community Relations Councils (JCRCs) and their national umbrella organization, the Jewish Council for Public Affairs (JCPA). They view their mission largely as demonstrating to groups beyond the Jewish community their devotion to those groups' interests. Increased criticism of Israel, or even of American Jews, from those groups often translates into yet more intense determination to demonstrate sympathy with them, even at the cost of tolerating hostility towards Israel or American Jews. An illustrative example is offered by Rebecca Schgallis, who describes a stonewalling by the local JCRC in response to Jewish parents' complaints of anti-Jewish and anti-Israel teachings and activities at Northern Virginia public schools. Schgallis observes, "We soon found that the JCRC was conflicted in its interests, and, rather than prioritizing fighting anti-Semitism, we found it to be more interested in currying favor with elected officials and promoting a 'progressive equity' agenda."[15] Also illustrative is David Bernstein's descrip-

---

15 Rebecca G. Schgallis, "Jewish Leadership Fails in Fairfax Country," in *Betrayal*, ed. Charles Jacobs and Avi Goldwasser (New York: Wicked Son, 2023), 208–219.

tion of his tenure, from January 2016 to February 2021, as JCPA's president and CEO.[16]

Shifts in Attitudes towards Israel among Israelis

Yet another factor that has led some American Jews to detach themselves from Israel over the past several decades has been intense criticism of Israel and its policies emanating from Israelis. There have always been Israelis voicing such criticism, but in the first decades of Israel's independence they were relatively few in number and generally marginalized. This changed dramatically in 1977 with the election of the first non-socialist government in Israel under the leadership of Menachem Begin.

Israelis, like Diaspora Jews, have not been immune to the corrosive psychological impact of being targeted by their neighbors—in their case, not as a minority community subject at times to anti-Jewish indictments, but as a Jewish state under chronic siege by surrounding states. Some always embraced the indictments of Israel's neighbors and insisted, for instance, after the 1967 war—ignoring the statements and actions emanating from the Palestinian leadership and from Arab states—that all would be well if Israel would only return to its pre-war lines. But the great majority had supported the government's position that peace could only come when Israel's Arab adversaries were prepared to recognize Israel's legitimacy and end their rejection of the Jewish state; the rejection reflected in the Arab League's post-1967 war Khartoum declaration of three no's: no recognition, no negotiation, no peace.

However, the Israeli Left's overwhelming support for this position was predicated not only on its obviously well-founded rationale but on the Left's identification with the leftist governments that had led Israel for the first three decades of its statehood. That changed with the accession of Begin and Likud. Soon, major elements of the Israeli Left began to argue that the new right-wing government was the obstacle to resolution of the Arab-Israeli conflict. It was too militant, too narrow-minded, and too distrustful of Israel's Arab neighbors. Peace would be possible if Israel only agreed to sufficient concessions that would translate the potential for peace

---

16 Bernstein, *Woke Antisemitism*, 62–91. See also Joanne Bregman, "JCPA 'Wokeness' Breeds Division," in *Betrayal*, ed. Charles Jacobs and Avi Goldwasser (New York: Wicked Son, 2023), 235–242.

into a reality. This view only grew within the Israeli Left over the next fifteen years, during which Likud either governed on its own or was senior partner or equal partner in governments of national unity. The stance was embraced by much of Israel's academic, cultural, and media elites. Their broad promotion of this perspective had an impact on the overwhelmingly left-leaning American Jewish community, elements of which readily fell in line with the perspective's vision of reality.

That vision, ultimately endorsed by about half of the Israeli electorate, paved the way for the Oslo Accords. In the 1992 Israeli election, Labor head Yitzhak Rabin ran on the traditional Labor platform: that Israel needed negotiating partners who eschewed terror and recognized the legitimacy of Israel as the nation state of the Jewish people, and that Israel could offer territorial compromises but would need to retain significant portions of the West Bank for its defense. (Rabin elaborated on the latter point, enumerating some of the areas Israel would need to hold, in his last speech in the Knesset prior to his assassination in 1995.) With Jordan having bowed out as a negotiating partner on behalf of the Palestinians, Rabin suggested internationally supervised elections in the territories to put in place a new Palestinian leadership made up of people living in the territories who would then enter negotiations with Israel.

But Rabin was soon the target of large-scale demonstrations by Israelis who insisted that Yasser Arafat and the Palestinian Liberation Organization (PLO) were the Palestinians' legitimate representatives and that Israel must negotiate with Arafat. Meanwhile, unbeknownst to Rabin, Yossi Beilin and Shimon Peres were overseeing negotiations with Arafat's agents in Oslo.

When informed of the Oslo track, Rabin acquiesced to its proceeding, and, in September 1993, he participated with Arafat in the ceremony on the White House lawn, formally launching the Oslo era. About half of Israel celebrated what it saw as the dawn of a long-sought era of peace, while the other half anticipated dire, bloody consequences of a dangerously misconceived course.

Evidence supporting the latter view but essentially unreported in Israel and largely ignored in the Jewish world was provided by Arafat in a speech that he gave on Jordanian television on the evening of the White House ceremony, after his famous handshake with Rabin. In the speech, he made clear that his objective remained Israel's annihilation.[17] He repeated the essence of his remarks at least a dozen times within weeks of the White House festivities.[18]

17 Foreign Broadcast Information Service, "Near East and South Asia, Daily Report Supplement, Israel-PLO Agreement," Tuesday, September 14, 1993, 4–5.
18 Efraim Karsh, Arafat's War (New York: Grove Press, 2003), 59.

Arafat and those around him consistently engaged in anti-Israel incitement, including calls for the state's destruction, in the weeks and months that followed. They enlisted the Palestinian media, mosques, and schools that came under their control to promote their anti-Israel agenda. But the Israeli government chose to downplay the incitement and defend Arafat.

Beyond incitement, there was also an increase in anti-Israel terror. Over the twenty-two months from Arafat's arrival in the territories in July 1994 until the fall of the Labor-Meretz government that had choreographed Oslo in May 1996, some 152 people were murdered in terror attacks. This rate of losses to terror was more than two-and-a-half times the rate in the twenty-six years from the 1967 war, when Israel had gained control of the West Bank and Gaza, to the start of Oslo. Yet the government responded to the terror largely as it did to the incitement. It downplayed the terror's significance, essentially exonerated Arafat, and exclusively blamed the Islamist organizations— despite Arafat's repeated praise of the terrorists and his refusal to clamp down on the Islamist groups in any meaningful way. Israel also continued to make concessions to Arafat, as in the signing of the Oslo II agreement in the fall of 1995.

While the incitement and terror, and the government's response, did not seem to generate a huge shift in Israeli opinion on Oslo, there was enough of a shift that opinion polls began to consistently show the government losing to Likud in a new election. This was the situation when Rabin was assassinated in November 1995. His murder triggered a wave of public sentiment in favor of the government, and the ruling coalition sought to capitalize on this by moving the elections scheduled for late 1996 up to May of that year. However, largely in response to ongoing incitement and terror in the intervening months, the election resulted in defeat of the Labor-Meretz coalition, which was replaced by a Likud government under Benjamin Netanyahu.

The growing second thoughts about Oslo also had some, albeit limited, impact on the elites that had almost unanimously embraced the accords. In 1997, senior *Haaretz* columnist Ari Shavit wrote, "In the early 90s . . . we, the enlightened Israelis, were infected with a messianic craze." Shavit then addressed the Left's hatred of Netanyahu, who at the time of the article had been in office for about a year and a half:

> Hatred of Netanyahu enables us to conveniently forget that before the bubble burst, we acted like fools. We fooled ourselves with illusions. We were bedazzled into committing a

collective act of messianic drunkenness. Hatred of Netanyahu also gives us a chance to forget that it was not the rise of Netanyahu that brought on the paralysis of Oslo but the paralysis of Oslo that brought on the rise of Netanyahu. The hatred permits us to keep harboring the notion that everything is really much more simple, that if we only pull back, if we only recognize Palestinian statehood . . . we would be able [once again] to breathe in that exhilarating, heady aroma of the end of history, the end of wars, the end of conflict.[19]

But Shavit was a rare exception among the "enlightened Israelis" of whom he was writing. Many of these people excoriated him for his new perspective on Oslo.

Like those Oslo enthusiasts in Israel that Shavit was addressing, many members of the American Jewish leadership who had embraced Oslo still retained their enthusiasm despite the anti-Israel incitement and terror promoted by Israel's "peace partners." Their views often differed dramatically from the Jewish rank and file. Evidence of the difference was offered by a poll conducted by the Indianapolis Jewish Community Relations Council in 1996, several months after the election of Netanyahu as prime minister. At the time of the poll, JCRCs across America, including the one in Indianapolis, together with the JCRC umbrella group (then called the National Jewish Community Relations Advisory Council), were all advancing an agenda that emphasized social action in a "liberal" vein, congruent with the desire to demonstrate "non-parochial" Jewish priorities. With regard to Israel, the JCRCs were claiming not only that Israel was now safe—the subtext of which was that American Jews were now freer to focus their energies on the JCRCs' "social justice" priorities—but that American Jews overwhelmingly concurred with this view and also overwhelmingly supported Oslo. However, the Indianapolis JCRC poll of community opinion indicated otherwise. About eighty percent of those questioned believed a Palestinian state would be a threat to Israel's security. Less than half felt that Israel should give up the West Bank, even with a viable peace. More than two-thirds said Arafat could not be trusted.[20]

---

19   Ari Shavit, "Why We Hate Him: The Real Reason," *Haaretz*, December 26, 1997.
20   See Tom Rose, "NJCRAC's Mistake," *Forward*, July 12, 1996.

Netanyahu was ultimately abandoned by elements of his coalition and forced into early elections in 1999. Some of his erstwhile supporters were dissatisfied that he had failed to stop Israeli compliance with Oslo-related concessions to Arafat despite the Palestinian Authority's reneging on its own repeatedly pledged Oslo commitments, including the promise to end incitement and terror. In addition, Netanyahu had acquiesced to further concessions. Others within his coalition saw clear indications that Arafat was preparing his people and forces for major new hostilities, and they believed it would be better for Israel if those hostilities occurred not on Likud's watch, when the Left would likely blame "right-wing intransigence" for the explosion, but under Labor, in which case the Right would rally to the government and there would be a much greater likelihood of national unity.

The 1999 election saw Netanyahu lose to the Labor-Meretz coalition led by Ehud Barak. Barak subsequently called for moving to final status negotiations with Arafat and convinced President Clinton to host those negotiations at Camp David in the summer of 2000. Palestinian preparations for war became even more evident and more intense in the months preceding the summit. At Camp David, Barak offered dramatic territorial concessions, far beyond anything Rabin had envisioned and anything thought prudent by Israel's defense establishment. But Arafat rejected the concessions as inadequate, turned down additional Israeli concessions proposed by President Clinton, offered no counter-proposals, and left Camp David. He clearly had no intention of signing any "end of conflict" agreement, no matter what Israel offered. A few months later Arafat launched his terror war against Israel.

Over the ensuing several years, more than a thousand Israelis were killed in the terror war and thousands more horribly maimed. The war led to a much more dramatic shift in Israeli opinion than the terror of the earlier Oslo years. A solid majority of Israelis were now convinced that there was no partner for peace. Additional defections from the "peace camp" occurred with Israel's unilateral withdrawal from Gaza in 2005 and the subsequent seizure of the area by Hamas, whose charter, as noted, calls not only for the annihilation of Israel but the murder of all the world's Jews. Gaza became not the venue for peaceful Palestinian development as anticipated by the advocates of unilateral withdrawal but rather the launching pad for thousands of rockets and missiles into Israel, attacks which—prior to October 7, 2023—triggered four wars in thirteen years. The broad shift in Israeli views has had an impact at the ballot box. Parties more focused on security, and more skeptical of any chance for progress towards genuine peace—given the Palestinian leadership's actions, declared objectives, and incitement in media, mosques, and schools—have generally prevailed since 2001.

But the shift in Israeli opinion does not mean that Oslo has lost its entire constituency. There remain Israelis who are convinced that, whatever the Palestinian leadership—whether the PA or Hamas—says or does, Israel is responsible for the absence of peace, and Israeli withdrawal from the territories (along with other concessions) would end the conflict. Israel's academic, media, and cultural elites are now even more overrepresented among those who cling to this stance. The perspectives of those elites are widely disseminated in the United States, and their views have an impact on American Jewish opinion that outweighs the actual representation of Israeli thinking. They also provide ammunition for those American Jewish leaders who, for reasons of their own domestic political predilections and agendas, are predisposed to identify with what had been the Israeli "peace" camp and have little sympathy for what is, in fact, a wide Israeli political consensus.

This preparedness to downplay or dismiss the Israeli consensus and the painful lessons that had engendered it, to cling instead to the conviction that peace could be had if only Israel were more forthcoming, is a revival of old, familiar themes. It is little different in its roots from the factors that shaped Felix Warburg's blindness to the plight of European Jewry before and during World War II and his insistence that the urgent quest for a Jewish state which would fulfill the League of Nations' promise of a national refuge reflected a "lust for power" and "a concept of Jewish life which is abhorrent." Those roots lie mainly in the fear of Zionist plans having negative impact on the status of American Jews.

To be sure, those in the American Jewish leadership and their like-minded followers who are so critical of Israel's leaders do not quite share the fears of American Jews of the first half of the twentieth century that support for a Jewish state might lead to a rollback of Jewish civic rights. But their attitudes vis-à-vis Israel are less the product of considerations of Israel's predicament than of similar domestic concerns.

As suggested earlier, this impulse to criticize Israeli leaders, not out of consideration of Israel's predicament but out of concern about the imagined impact of Israeli policies on the well-being of the American Jewish community, has only increased in the face of the recent burgeoning antisemitism in America. It is linked to the delusional wish to construe the antisemitism, particularly that coming from the Left, as primarily directed against Israel, and to blame not the haters but the Jewish state. And it can be found even among Jews genuinely concerned with Israel's well-being.

It is the perspective reflected, for example, in Gary Rosenblatt's article discussed in Chapter One. Again, the piece appeared early in 2016 under the title "Frustration with Israel Growing Here at Home." Rosenblatt writes of the discomfort of many American Jews, including community leaders, with increasing criticism of Israel in America, and their blaming Israeli policies for the problem. He ultimately makes clear that he shares this view and is sympathetic to the impulse of communal leaders eager to convince Netanyahu, then prime minister, to produce "a plan, any plan" to move the Israeli-Palestinian impasse forward and thereby, to their imagining, assuage the growing hostile views of Israel in America.

But, once more, the falling away from Israel among some in the Jewish community, including in its leadership, is much less a reaction to Israeli policy than a function of those American Jewish circles identifying with, and wanting to propitiate, elements in the wider society who have increasingly adopted anti-liberal, "progressive" world views, including a hostility to Israel. This is also why those same American Jewish circles are so receptive to, indeed enamored of, Israeli voices that—unlike the clear majority of their fellow citizens—cling to the Oslo fantasies of yore and blame Israel first and always.

Gerald Steinberg is head of NGO Monitor, which follows and calls out the myriad NGOs dedicated to pushing anti-Israel distortions of reality and often to aiding groups that pursue Israel's destruction. Steinberg touches on the above assessment of the American scene in a response to Rosenblatt entitled "Why Israel Is Frustrated with American Jewish Leaders: Fringe Israeli Voices that Polarize and Demonize Our Society are Given Legitimacy and Resources in America" (published by Rosenblatt, to his credit, in the *Jewish Week* on January 27, 2016). Steinberg notes that, "Like most Israelis, I also hope for a peace plan, but not any plan, and certainly not one that will bring us yet another disaster when it fails... So no, 'any plan' that helps Israel's PR among liberal [sic] students, but makes our security situation even worse, is not better than the status quo."

This delusional blaming and criticizing of Israel is widespread among people in respected positions in the community that are basically supportive of the state, such as Rosenblatt. It is not surprising that it would be still more common and more intense among Jews who are ensconced in environments critical of Israel and who are even more predisposed to value ingratiating themselves with their professional peers over insisting on an honest reality-based assessment of the Jewish state.

Tony Judt held an endowed professorship in history at New York University. In 2003, he published an article in the *New York Review of Books* entitled "Israel: The Alternative."[21] At that time, the suicide-bomber terror war launched by Arafat was still raging. Yet Judt equates Arafat and Ariel Sharon (then prime minister), ridicules the notion that the current Israeli-Palestinian difficulties were "all Arafat's fault" and characterizes the American president as Israel's dupe. He faults Israel for not dismantling settlements and returning to its 1967 "borders" (which were not borders but merely 1948 cease-fire lines) and recognizes that its doing so is unlikely now, given the existence of settlements in the territories. His solution: a binational state. He argues that, in any case, Israel is an anachronism: "The very idea of a 'Jewish state,' a state in which Jews and the Jewish religion have exclusive privileges from which non-Jewish citizens are forever excluded is rooted in another time and place. . . . [The world] has moved on, a world of . . . open frontiers, and international law."

Judt packs an impressive number of distortions of reality into his assertions. He would not be able to name any legal privileges enjoyed by Jews but not by Arab Israelis in the Jewish state because there are none. He claims that a state defined by religion is an anachronism; but, for example, every Arab state, and indeed every Muslim state is defined this way, and each does, in fact, permit non-Muslims only lesser privileges, if any at all. But Judt does not suggest that any of them should be reconfigured, nor does he condemn them as anachronisms.

Additional distortions of reality are piled on. Judt claims that UN resolutions require Israel's return to its pre-1967 lines. But Security Council Resolution 242, the main relevant document, calls not for such a return but rather to a withdrawal to "agreed and recognized boundaries." He suggests that America went to war with Iraq for Israel's sake, a common assertion by anti-Israel circles in the States. But, in fact, Israeli leaders were typically against the war, anticipating—correctly, as time has shown—that Saddam's overthrow would simply empower Iran. He argues that American support for Israel had undermined its standing with the Arab states, but America's years as the dominant and most respected power in the Middle East have largely coincided with its alliance with and support of Israel. In pushing for his binational solution, Judt points to European nations having become multicultural. He does not talk of religious minorities in the Middle East, who have all been under siege, with several subjected to campaigns of genocide.

---

21 Tony Judt, "Israel: The Alternative," *New York Review of Books*, September 25, 2003.

Nor does he note the genocidal agendas that had characterized (and continue to characterize) every Palestinian leadership. But fear not; Judt does concede that, "The security of Jews and Arabs alike would need to be guaranteed by international force."

Why all these dishonest and carelessly assembled arguments against Israel from a seemingly respected historian? The answer is that they are, in large part, irrelevant to his genuine grievance against the Jewish state, which only emerges in the twenty-second paragraph of "Israel: The Alternative":

> Today, non-Israeli Jews feel themselves once again exposed to criticism and vulnerable to attack for things they didn't do. But this time it is a Jewish state, not a Christian one, which is holding them hostage for its own actions. Diaspora Jews cannot influence Israeli policies, but they are implicitly identified with them, not least by Israel's own insistent claims upon their allegiance. The behavior of a self-described Jewish state affects the way everyone else looks at Jews. The increased incidence of attacks on Jews in Europe and elsewhere is primarily attributable to misdirected efforts, often by young Muslims, to get back at Israel. The depressing truth is that Israel's current behavior is not just bad for America, though it surely is. It is not even just bad for Israel itself, as many Israelis silently acknowledge. The depressing truth is that Israel today is bad for the Jews.

It transpires that Judt's real grievance against Israel is that he as a Jew feels Israel has tarred his standing in the world; presumably, particularly with those with whom he identifies, such as his colleagues at NYU.

It is a perspective shared by other Jews for whom the existence of the Jewish state and well-being of its citizens count for less than their own comfort, and who see the latter suffering from the former. It is the mindset captured in the 2010 statement in the *Jerusalem Post* on the occasion of Judt's death and cited at the beginning of this chapter:

> The death of Tony Judt, historian of contemporary Europe, offers an opportunity to revisit a case of strongly anti-Zionist sentiments held by a prominent Jewish intellectual . . . [I]t was the New York University lecturer's polemical essays and public statements against Zionism, and his rejection of the legitimacy of the Jewishness of the State of Israel, that thrust

him onto the public stage. In a much-cited October 2003
essay in *The New York Review of Books*, Judt called to dismantle
the state and to replace it with "a single, integrated, bi-national
state" between the Jordan River and the Mediterranean
Sea—a recipe for national suicide for the sovereign Jewish
entity . . . "The behavior of a self-described Jewish state affects
the way everyone else looks at Jews," wrote Judt. His solution?
Do away with [Israel].

There are, of course, numerous Jews in the public arena today who, like Judt,
call for the dissolution of Israel and creation of a binational state. Some are
less forthcoming than Judt in acknowledging, as a spur to their own attacks
on the Jewish state, the desire to ingratiate themselves with anti-Israel circles.
But such a desire seems essential to account for their willingness to propound
those extreme distortions of reality with which they defend their attacks on
Israel and, even more remarkably, their blithe indifference to the dire fate that
would befall Israel's Jews should they submit to a binational arrangement.

Two popular proponents of this course are Peter Beinart and Judith
Butler. Butler has characterized the October 7 massacre as armed resistance,
choosing to construe rape and the incineration of children as consistent
with that characterization, and has suggested the attack was "right." Butler
has also declared that, "It is not a terrorist attack and it's not an antisemitic
attack." There is, of course, no acknowledgment of Hamas's explicitly proclaimed goal of annihilating all Jews. Butler is more focused on creating, via
a binational state, the conditions that would make that goal more feasible,
and Butler's distortions of reality are in the service of advancing a program
of annihilation that appeals to a subset of Jew-haters with whom Butler
apparently identifies.[22]

The same can be said of Beinart. He titled a January 2025 opinion piece in
the *New York Times* "States Don't Have a Right to Exist. People Do." The title
captures, of course, his argument that Israel has no overarching right to exist,
and he invokes in the piece numerous false analogies to prop up his thesis. But
the title also exposes the sickness in Beinart's program. He at once declares that
people have a right to exist yet advocates a course that, given the stated aims of
Israel's Palestinian enemies, would clearly entail depriving seven million people,

---

22 Jane Prinsley, "Outrage as Influential Feminist Academic Judith Butler calls October 7
Murder and Rape 'Resistance,'" *Jewish Chronicle*, March 7, 2024.

the Jews of Israel, of that right. But that is, again, the objective of Jew-haters, among them some whose approval Beinart apparently wishes to cultivate.[23]

American Jews, Israel, and the American Left

Even with the recent rise of antisemitism in America, polls of American opinion consistently show high levels of support for Israel. A poll conducted by Douglas Schoen and Carly Cooperman in January 2025 showed 70% of Americans supported Israel's right to defend itself. This included 79% of Republicans, 65% of Democrats, and 65% of Independents. In addition, 76% of Republicans, 57% of Independents, and 53% of Democrats agreed that, "the U.S. should remain a steadfast ally of Israel and fully support it in a war with Iran."[24] A Harvard-Harris poll, also dating from January 2025, revealed 79% of Americans supporting Israel over Hamas.[25]

Why then, one might ask, the concerns among some Jews, particularly among Jewish leaders, of Israeli policies creating difficulties for Jews in America? One factor, again, is the widespread wish to believe that the increased antisemitism is secondary to anger at Israel, which generates the impulse to critique Israeli policies. Another possible factor is that even some of those in the American Jewish community attuned to the support in America for Israel may nevertheless worry that that support could slip away if Israel does not make what they consider the "right" moves. But a more valid answer relates these American Jewish concerns to American Jews', and to an even greater extent their leaders', identification with the political Left in America, and even more so with academic, media, and cultural elites that are almost monochromatically leftist. They are sensitive to the views of those groups much more than to the views of the population more broadly and are swayed by those elites' anti-Israel predilections, which have only grown more intense in recent years. Those groups, too, generally insist that Israel bears most of the responsibility for the absence of peace in the Middle East and that peace would follow if Israel would only grant Palestinians their "rights."

---

23 Peter Beinart, "States Don't Have a Right to Exist. People Do," *New York Times*, January 27, 2025.
24 Douglas Schoen and Carly Cooperman, "Opinion: Polling Reveals Americans' Widespread Bipartisan Support for Israel," *Hill*, January 27, 2025.
25 David Israel, "Harris-Harvard Poll: 79% of Americans Continue to Support Israel Against Hamas," *Jewish Press*, January 20, 2025.

This ongoing identification by much of the Jewish community, and even more so by its leaders, with institutions, groups, and causes associated with the Left is on vivid display in today's America. So too is their reluctance to acknowledge developments on the Left inimical to Jewish interests. As noted in previous chapters, and as pointed out by Rabbi Hertzberg with regard to the 1960s, the Anti-Defamation League has typically been much readier to call out right-wing antisemitism than that emanating from the Left. The ADL has in recent years repeatedly and strongly condemned what can be seen as a resurgence of neo-Nazi and other extreme Right antisemitic groups in the United States. But such groups, however vile their rhetoric and their behavior, hardly represent a greater threat in terms of the numbers of their followers and their penetration into mainstream society than the no less ugly Jew-hatred coming from the other end of the political spectrum.

Louis Farrakhan is without doubt the spewer of antisemitic invective with the widest following in America today. His apologists extend to members of the Congressional Black Caucus and other prominent mainstream figures. While the ADL has issued many statements attacking Farrakhan for his Jew-baiting, it has rarely taken issue with his many high-profile enablers, who are typically Black and associated with the political Left. A rare instance when it has connected Farrakhan with a prominent figure was when he had indicated support for then presidential candidate Donald Trump. The ADL did so under the headline "Louis Farrakhan Joins List of Extremists Praising Donald Trump."[26]

One prominent Black leftist who has supported Farrakhan and who has himself spewed anti-Jewish invective and been involved in anti-Jewish violence, including acts that led to a number of deaths, is Al Sharpton. Yet the ADL under Jonathan Greenblatt, rather than taking issue with Sharpton, has effectively embraced him as an ally against the Right, as noted, for example, by Liel Liebowitz in "The Mind-Bendingly Insane, Completely Craven, Utterly Unconscionable Redemption of Al Sharpton: You're Not Confused. The ADL is Becoming as Bad as You Think."[27]

26 Oren Segal, "Louis Farrakhan Joins List of Extremists Praising Donald Trump," ADL, February 29, 2016, https://www.adl.org/resources/article/louis-farrakhan-joins-list-extremists-praising-donald-trump.
27 Liel Liebowitz, "The Mind-Bendingly Insane, Completely Craven, Utterly Unconscionable Redemption of Al Sharpton: You're Not Confused. The ADL is Becoming as Bad as You Think." *Tablet Magazine*, August 23, 2020.

American campuses, overwhelmingly dominated by the Left, have col-
lectively become the American institution most associated with attacks on
Jews. Anti-Jewish violence on campuses emanates from faculty as well as
student groups. Jewish students are repeatedly subjected to marginalization,
intimidation, verbal abuse, and even physical abuse. Yet, while the ADL, as
discussed in Chapter Three, has taken some steps since October 7, 2023,
to address the crisis on campus, its activities in this regard have been very
limited. Hillel's efforts also continue to fall short. And none other among the
legacy Jewish organizations has stepped up to fill the void.

As noted earlier, in December 2017, four imams in the United States
called for attacks on Jews, three in sermons in their mosques and the fourth
in a Facebook posting. While the incidents drew criticism from mainstream
Jewish organizations, including the ADL, the critique almost invariably failed
to note that such antisemitic rhetoric is standard fare in these imams' countries of origin and throughout much of the Muslim world.

One might ask why the imams' hateful bigotry would be considered left-
wing rather than right-wing. The answer lies in the fact that much of the
American Left has made defense of Muslims in America, including Muslim
groups with radical Islamist agendas and affiliations, a political issue. They
have sought to cast those to the right of themselves, and those critical of
elements of the Muslim community, as nativist bigots preying on American
Muslims. Many in the Jewish community, particularly in the mainstream
leadership, have readily embraced this formula and sought to fashion
relations with Muslims in a manner consistent with this comprehension.
A good illustration of the phenomenon, depicting the Boston area Jewish
leadership's response to a local mosque with extremist affiliations, is Ilya
Feoktistov's *Terror in the Cradle of Liberty: How Boston Became a Center of
Islamic Extremism.*[28]

Similarly, the Left, including President Obama during his tenure and many
of those around him, has repeatedly spoken of the depredations emanating
from Islamophobia in America, and segments of the Jewish community have
picked up this theme. Yet, while some incidents of Muslims being targeted
have occurred, and any such episode is one too many, in fact, according to
FBI statistics, it is Jews who are overwhelmingly the primary targets of
religion-based hate crimes in America. In 2016, the last full year of Obama's

---

28   Ilya Feoktistov, *Terror in the Cradle of Liberty: How Boston Became a Center for Islamic
Extremism* (New York: Encounter Books, 2019).

presidency, Jews were the victims of 54% of such crimes; Muslims the victims of 24%.[29] (Statistics for 2022, the last full year before the upsurge in antisemitism following the October 7 massacre, showed 51.9% of religion-based hate crimes were against Jews, while Muslims were the targets of 9.6% of such crimes.)[30] Those on the Left inveighing against Islamophobia, again including the former president and the people around him, have virtually never acknowledged this reality. Nor has the mainstream Jewish leadership taken issue with their failure to do so or, all too often, even noted what the statistics actually showed.

When the leadership, and much of the community, have been so weak in addressing anti-Jewish rhetoric and actions, as well as other threats, coming from the Left, when they have persisted in their determination to identify with the Left and march with the Left no matter what stands inimical to American Jews the Left embraces, it is hardly surprising that, as the Left targets Israel, the response is grossly inadequate. The inclination among much of American Jewry, and particularly among community leaders, is less to challenge the Left than to wish Israel would shape its policies to accommodate leftist criticism—whether that criticism comes from the academy, or elements of the Democrat Party, or the mainstream media, or the so-called "liberal" churches. As noted earlier with regard to the ADL's limited steps to address campus antisemitism and antizionism in the wake of October 7, there has been, since the massacre, some positive movement in the Jewish organizational response to the threats facing both the American Jewish community and Israel. But the response continues falling far short of the need.

Moreover, as discussed in Chapter Three, the dramatic increase in antisemitism emanating from the Red-Green-Black alliance in America has amplified the self-deluding impulse among many in the Jewish leadership and among significant numbers of their followers to construe the burgeoning antisemitism as secondary to attacks on Israel—this despite all the evidence that American Jews are not merely a secondary target. The old, recurring impulse of Jews to blame other Jews, to blame Jews on the other side of some political or social or religious divide, for antisemitism simply reinforces this

29 "2016 Hate Crime Statistics," Uniform Crime Reporting Program, https://www.fbi.gov/news/stories/2016-hate-crime-statistics.
30 "Which groups have experienced an increase in hate crimes?," USAFacts, December 14, 2023, https://usafacts.org/articles/which-groups-have-experienced-an-increase-in-hate-crimes/.

predilection to appease the attackers on the Left by joining them in their critiques of Israel.

An example of this phenomenon is provided by Reform Judaism leader Rabbi Rick Jacobs in a letter he addressed to "Dear Reform Students" at the end of the 2023–2024 academic year. (The letter is discussed in greater detail later.) Jacobs describes and reflects on his visit to the Columbia University campus during the anti-Israel and antisemitic demonstrations. He ends his missive with advice to students going forward. In doing so, he interprets what has transpired solely in terms of events in Israel and Gaza, with some implied criticism of Israel, and fails even to consider the campus demonstrations as attacks on American Jews irrespective of their links to Israel.

With regard to Israel-attackers on the Left, one would think that the realities of the Jewish state—with its democratic institutions that compare well to similar structures in any of the states of the democratic West, its maintaining of an uncompromised open society even in the face of persistent existential threats, its besiegement by dictatorial and totalitarian nations and transnational and subnational groups explicitly dedicated to its annihilation and the extermination of its people—would naturally draw to the Jewish state the sympathy of "liberal" opinion in the West. But, again, the political Left in the West, including in America, has largely drifted away from "liberal" positions to a post-liberal leftism. In this new leftism, promotion and defense of democracy and individual rights count for less than criticism of the West for its colonial past, sympathy for third world anti-Western movements of whatever stripe, and moral relativism; positions justified in the name of moving beyond Western supremacism and racism and toward "international solidarity." Those who subscribe to this new leftism have tended to identify more with the "third world" attackers of Israel—and with the international institutions that those attackers, by virtue of their numbers and international clout, have been able to subvert to support of their anti-Israel agenda—than with the Middle East's lone democracy and its struggle for survival.

But many American Jews, in the face of this clash between the contemporary ideological Left that has gained increasing sway in the Democrat Party in recent years and the well-being of Israel, have embraced a cognitive dissonance. It manifests itself in a simultaneous commitment, in their own minds, both to Israel's well-being and to traditional political affiliations and agendas, and in a chosen blindness to the internal contradictions. They, as well as those Jews less concerned with Israel's well-being, are unprepared to question their loyalty to the political Left. They are unwilling to note that the American Left has widely abandoned liberal positions and embraced an anti-liberal, and antisemitic, post-liberal leftism. They do not point out the lies and hypocrisy of the Left's attacks on Israel. Rather, they prefer to give credence to critiques of Israel, which they choose to construe as somehow more benign than they genuinely are, and to thereby preserve their delusions that the leftists are correct and the solution to anti-Jewish and anti-Israel sentiment lies in Israeli reform.

Also consistent with this pattern, much of American Jewry, including many of its leaders, has tolerated and even supported American leftist whitewashing of the Palestinian leadership while casting Israel's policies as the obstacles to peace. Mahmoud Abbas has repeatedly asserted that Jews have no historic connection with the Holy Land, that they are merely alien invaders, and that he will never recognize the legitimacy of a Jewish state. He has declared that he will never give up the Palestinian "right of return," the supposed right of Palestinian refugees and their descendants to settle in Israel. He has incited violence against Israelis in his media and mosques and has taught in his schools that the highest calling for Palestinian children is to dedicate themselves to Israel's destruction. He has spent hundreds of millions of dollars yearly promoting terrorism and supporting terrorists and their families. He has complained about Jews violating the Temple Mount with their filthy feet, insisted the site is holy only to Muslims, and called upon his people to defend it from supposed Jewish depredations. He has walked away from every peace plan put forward by Israeli or American administrations, failed to make any counter-proposals, and made clear there is no plan to which—if it is cast as a final, end-of-conflict, arrangement—he will agree. He has made clear that he, like Arafat, will regard any arrangement as just a step towards the ultimate dissolution of Israel and establishment of a Muslim state on all the land between the Jordan and the Mediterranean.

Yet, during the Obama administration, the president and those around him characterized Abbas as the "moderate" and the Israeli government as the problem in its failure to make the concessions that would satisfy Abbas and win peace. Many American Jews, again most particularly community leaders, chose not to challenge this gross and bigoted distortion of reality and hoped that Israel would change course and somehow deliver those magical, peace-assuring concessions. This stance was adopted even by many people who were, in their own way, devoted to Israel and its well-being.

This pattern has continued in recent years. Taylor Force was a graduate of West Point, a veteran of the Iraq and Afghanistan wars. He was visiting Israel in March 2016, with a study group as part of his work on a graduate degree at Vanderbilt University, when he was murdered in Tel Aviv by a Palestinian terrorist. The Taylor Force Act was subsequently introduced in Congress to forbid the granting of federal funds to the Palestinians until the Palestinian Authority ended its "pay to slay" policy of providing stipends to terrorists who attacked Israelis and others and to the families of deceased terrorists. The Act was passed by Congress and signed into law in March 2018. Such PA payments have been exceeding 300 million dollars a year, with amounts to any individual terrorist and terrorist family determined by how many Israelis and others the terrorist had killed and injured. Abbas's reaction to the law was to insist that nothing would sway the PA from continuing such payments, and indeed nothing has. Yet, immediately on assuming office, President Biden declared his intention to resume subsidizing the Palestinian Authority, ignoring or circumventing the law. He subsequently gave the Palestinians more than a billion dollars.[31]

Biden also resumed payments to UNWRA, the UN agency uniquely dedicated to providing services to Palestinian "refugees" (that is, refugees from the 1947–1948 war and their descendants). As noted in the previous chapter, UNWRA's responsibilities have included educating young Palestinians in schools in UN-administered refugee camps, where, for some seventy years, students have been taught to hate Jews and devote their lives to Israel's destruction. UNRWA has also allowed its facilities to be used as recruiting and training grounds and armories for terrorists, and its teachers and other staff include members of Hamas. It was because of this record of abetting terrorism and advocating Israel's annihilation that the first Trump administration had ended American funding to UNWRA. But the Biden administration resumed financing the agency, providing it with more than 600 million dollars in grants[32] before halting the subsidies in the face of revelations that UNRWA employees in Gaza were involved in the October 7, 2023, massacre and that many dozens of employees subsequently celebrated the massacre. Israel's troops that entered Gaza after October 7 also discovered unexpectedly extensive Hamas infrastructure and weaponry in and under UNRWA facilities.

---

31 See, for example, Daniel Greenfield, "After Biden Sent $1 Billion to the PLO, Israeli Deaths Rose 900%," Jewish News Syndicate, February 15, 2023.

32 See, for example, "US Contributions to UNRWA in 2021–2022 Are Key to Agency's Ability to Operate," United Nations Relief and Works Agency for Palestine Refugees in the Near East, July 19, 2022.

The Biden administration demonstrated its hostility towards Israel and its people in other ways as well. For example, it appointed individuals virulently hostile to Israel to positions dealing directly with issues vital to Israel's security.

Hadi Amr was national coordinator of the anti-Israel Middle East Justice Network in 2002 when he said of his work, "I was inspired by the Palestinian intifada"; that is, he was inspired by Arafat's terror war of suicide bombings of buses, restaurants, and other locales that killed over a thousand Israelis.[33] Amr also expressed warm feelings for Hamas, was professionally affiliated with Qatar—a Muslim Brotherhood state and major supporter of Hamas— and has urged American outreach to Hamas. Biden, in the early days of his administration, appointed Amr to be deputy assistant secretary of state for Israel-Palestine.[34] In November 2022, Amr was assigned the newly created position of special representative for Palestinian affairs. Maher Bitar, Biden's senior director for intelligence on the National Security Council, was another appointee with a history of anti-Israel activism that was given a position having immediate relevance to Israeli security issues.

Biden, after taking office, tried to revive Obama's Iran deal, which provided a path for that country to develop, with the signatories' approval, a nuclear weapons arsenal, even as Iran continued to declare its determination to annihilate Israel. Biden tolerated Iranian violation of numerous trade sanctions, in the interest of winning Iran over to agreeing to a new nuclear deal, but thereby provided additional opportunities for Iran to finance its terror-supporting projects. He also arranged the release of embargoed overseas funds to Iran, further enabling the mullahs to sustain and expand their terror operations.

Biden selected Robert Malley as his point man for negotiations with the Iranians. Malley had been a member of President Clinton's Middle East negotiating team during the 2000 Camp David talks with Ehud Barak and Yasser Arafat. Clinton, after Camp David, had blamed Arafat—who rejected all of his and Barak's offers without making any counter-proposals—for the breakdown of the talks. But Malley subsequently insisted that Clinton was wrong, that the fault for failure of the talks lay with Israel and not Arafat. In fact, Malley and his family had a longstanding and close personal relationship with Arafat.[35] His efforts in talks with Iran on behalf of the Biden administration yielded no

33 Daniel Greenfield, "The Problem with Hady Amr," Jewish News Syndicate, February 4, 2021.
34 Ibid.
35 See, for example, Alex Safian, "Robert Malley and US Policy on Israel," Committee for Accuracy in Middle East Reporting and Analysis, March 11, 2015.

agreement despite reports of major American concessions, and Malley, under circumstances that have never been publicly clarified, was relieved of his duties apparently over questions of security breaches. But the administration had clearly been comfortable with having as their lead negotiator an advocate of extensive accommodation of the Iranians and someone who has never exhibited any concern about the threats a nuclear Iran would pose to Israel. One can cite additional Biden appointments to sensitive positions of people with histories of hostility to Israel and indeed hostility to Jews in general.

As noted in the previous chapter, Biden provided strong support for Israel in the immediate wake of Hamas's murderous rampage of October 7, 2023. But he encountered much opposition to this stance not only from progressive and Islamist elements of the Democrat Congressional delegation and within the wider Democrat constituency but also from the many members of his administration hostile to Israel. In addition, Biden daily received warnings from Democrat Party strategists that his support for Israel in its campaign to dismantle Hamas and derail its genocidal agenda would cost him the votes of progressives, of Muslim Americans, and of young people in the coming 2024 election.

In response to these pressures, Biden was soon taking steps that undercut Israel's war efforts. Even before Israel launched its ground campaign in Gaza, Biden was urging it to avoid a major incursion and settle for hit-and-run raids against the terror organization, a strategy that would have left Hamas essentially intact. He similarly voiced opposition to every major Israeli advance in the war. Israeli steps to accommodate Biden's objections slowed Israel's advance, giving Hamas greater opportunities to regroup and consequently extending the war at the cost of more Israeli and Palestinian lives.

Biden made a particular effort to stop Israel from going into Rafah, Gaza's southernmost town at the border with Egypt. He threatened to cut off weapons shipments to Israel if it proceeded into Rafah. Israel eventually did so after a several months' delay and seized the Philadelphi corridor between Gaza and Egypt, through which and under which Hamas had long smuggled armaments from Iran. Closing this conduit was vital to defeating the terror organization. The Biden administration, as threatened, subsequently suspended some arms shipments and slowed delivery of others.

The administration also pressured Israel in other arenas. Hezbollah had begun cross-border attacks on Israel's north on October 8, the day after the Hamas invasion and slaughter in the south of the country. Hezbollah stated it had done so in support of Hamas. It continued rocket, missile, drone, and

RPG attacks throughout the following months. More than 60,000 Israelis were forced to abandon their homes in the north and seek refuge elsewhere. Yet, as in Gaza, Biden attempted to prevent an Israeli ground incursion into southern Lebanon. Again, Israel had no real choice but to defy administration pressures if it hoped to end the Hezbollah assault, reestablish some deterrence, and return its citizens to their homes.

In addition, as Israel was making very substantive headway in dismantling the Hezbollah terror resources in southern Lebanon and advancing its campaign against Hezbollah elsewhere in the country, the Biden administration—by various threats involving further withholding of arms supplies and undercutting of the Jewish state in international fora—forced Israel into a very disadvantageous ceasefire. The terms of the ceasefire entailed Israel's total withdrawal from southern Lebanon in sixty days, Hezbollah left in a position to reestablish itself on Israel's northern border, and limitations on Israel's ability to respond to ongoing Hezbollah threats.

Consistent with Biden's presidency-long efforts to court Iran with the aim of getting it to join an amended nuclear agreement—which would again allow Iran to pursue nuclear weapons with the signatories' acquiescence—he pressured Israel not to respond to Iran's April 1 missile and drone attack on the Jewish state. Israel did attack, but only minimally, hitting one element of Iran's air defense system. When, in October, Iran again attacked, this time causing greater damage to Israel, Biden insisted that any Israeli response not target either Iran's nuclear facilities or its oil industry. The former caveat was particularly contrary to Israel's essential interests, as Iran's nuclear program presents the greatest threat to the Jewish state.

Another step taken by Biden to assuage anti-Israel cadres in the Democrat congressional delegation, in the executive bureaucracy, and in the party's constituency was repeatedly casting the events of October 7 and the subsequent war in Gaza as an opportunity to create finally a Palestinian state in the West Bank, East Jerusalem, and Gaza. He pushed this even as Israelis overwhelmingly realized that the October 7 massacre proved the deadly danger of having long tolerated the presence on their borders of leaders who actively promoted the annihilation of Israel and the genocide of its people and demonstrated the existential threat that would be posed by giving them and their indoctrinated constituents a state.

Still further steps to appease those hostile to Israel were imposing sanctions on some individuals and institutions associated with the Israeli presence in the West Bank. Some of the sanctioned targets were rogue figures, but others were not. In addition, accusations were made of "settlers" attacking Palestinians when the facts of the alleged provocations most often indicated otherwise. These measures, and other related policies, seemed to reflect administration efforts to undermine the Israeli presence in the West Bank; a reprise of Obama administration policy. Both presidents—Obama more emphatically than Biden—sought to cast that presence as an illegitimate expansionist right-wing Israeli undertaking. They both ignored the reality that a broad consensus of Israelis see retention of particular strategic locations in the territory as vital to Israel's survival; locations partially enumerated by Yitzhak Rabin in his last speech in the Knesset prior to his assassination.[36]

Amid the news coverage of all these steps taken by the Biden administration to compromise Israel's security and aid its enemies in the service of assuaging anti-Israel cadres among congressional Democrats, administration officials, and Democrat constituents, one did not see stories about Jewish pushback. There was virtually nothing on Jewish leaders pointing out that Jewish voters—long predominantly Democrat voters—cannot be taken for granted when they are told that elements of their party leadership are willing to sacrifice Israel's, and the Jewish community's, well-being to placate anti-Jewish blocs. Indeed, there was scant evidence of such pushback. And why, then, would party operatives who advocate abandonment of the Jews and of Israel rethink their course when there appeared to be no downside to continuing in the same course?

Far from pushback, many American Jews, and particularly community leaders, eager to resolve the dissonance between their concern for Israel and their devotion to the political Left, have persisted in old patterns of willful blindness. They either ignore the bias currently epidemic on the Left, including within the Democrat Party, or choose to construe it as essentially, and as not entirely inappropriately, directed at Israel, not at American Jews, and as a problem that can be addressed by Israeli reforms. Blaming Israel in the face of attacks from the Left is even more common among those American Jews less concerned about Israel's well-being, or whose earlier attachment to Israel has been undermined by their sensitivity to attacks on the Jewish state from quarters with which they identify. Such individuals are even more inclined to blame Israel for American Jewry's current problems and to insist that those problems must be addressed through Israeli reforms.

---

36 See, for example, Kenneth Levin, "Biden's Israeli Ambassador vs. Yitzhak Rabin on Israel's Security," Jewish News Syndicate, March 27, 2022.

The previous chapter discussed how the recent tolerance within the Democrat Party for explicitly antisemitic rhetoric and actions by party officials has had virtually no impact on American Jewish voting patterns. It would hardly be surprising then that anti-Israel rhetoric and actions, and anti-Israel attitudes among Democrat loyalists, would likewise have no significant impact on Jewish voting patterns. A February 2022 Gallup poll, looking at where American sympathies lie in the Israeli-Palestinian conflict, found that among Republicans 77% sympathized more with the Israelis, 13% with the Palestinians. In contrast, among Democrats 40% expressed greater sympathy with the Israelis, 38% with the Palestinians.[37] A Gallup poll released a year later, in March 2023, showed support for the Palestinians among Democrats had increased to 49%, markedly greater than that for Israel, which had declined slightly to 39%. Among Republicans, sympathy for Israel increased marginally to 78% while that for the Palestinians declined to 11%.[38] The 2024 presidential election, coming after all the previous year's escalated outpouring of Jew-hatred as well as murderous hostility to Israel from major constituencies of the Left, did, as previously noted, entail some shift in Jewish voting in favor of the Republican candidate. But the size of the shift, while substantial in some areas of the country, did not reflect a dramatic break from prior overall voting patterns.

Mainstream American Jewish Bodies and Israel

Rabbi Rick Jacobs, president of the Union for Reform Judaism, is, as previously suggested, another prominent American Jewish leader whose perspectives regarding Israel are shaped largely by attitudes on the American Left and by the American Jewish embrace of those attitudes. Jacobs has been almost invariably critical of Prime Minister Netanyahu and his policies. At times, that criticism focused largely on the issue of prayer at the Western Wall in Jerusalem. In January 2016, after years of negotiations, the Israeli government agreed to establish a so-called "egalitarian" prayer area at the Wall, outside the control of the Orthodox rabbinate and free of its strictures. But in June 2017 the government froze implementation of the plan, triggering angry reactions

37 Lydia Saad, "Americans Still Pro-Israel, though Palestinian Support Grows," Gallup Poll News Service, March 17, 2022.
38 Lydia Saad, "Democrats' Sympathies in Middle East Shift to Palestinians," Gallup Poll News Service, March 16, 2023.

from, particularly, American Reform and other non-Orthodox circles, including from Jacobs. Jacobs's unhappiness with Netanyahu, however, predates the Western Wall controversy and goes well beyond issues related to treatment of the Reform movement in Israel.

Reporting for the *Jerusalem Post* on the Union for Reform Judaism's biennial convention in 2015, Elliot Jager noted the prominence of "calls for more vigorous criticism of Israeli policies . . . and heightened activism for social justice." Of Rabbi Jacobs's keynote address, Jager observed: "[He] could not identify a single policy of Benjamin Netanyahu's government that his movement could heartily embrace. For him, 'asking Jews around the world only to wave the flag of Israel and to support even the most misguided policies of its leaders drives a wedge between the Jewish soul and the Jewish state. It is beyond counterproductive.'"[39] And Jacobs has made clear that among those "misguided policies" are, to his perception, the Israeli government's failure to do more to achieve a solution to the conflict with the Palestinians.

The great majority of Israelis may feel—having paid a steep price in blood for previous concessions in Israel's search for peace—that there is no partner on the other side, whether the PA or Hamas, with whom a genuine peace can be negotiated at this time. Israelis may now overwhelmingly believe both Palestinian leaderships when they declare that they are not interested in peace with Israel and that their goal remains Israel's demise. But Jacobs, and many others in the Reform leadership, moved by a frame of reference not Israeli, somehow construe this Israeli perspective as representing "a wedge between the Jewish soul and the Jewish state."[40]

As noted earlier, while much of the Reform membership shares Jacobs's views regarding Israel, there are many Reform Jews, including among the movement's leading figures, who do not. In contrast to Jacobs's perception of Israel's supposed failures in peacemaking as inconsistent with "the Jewish soul," Rabbi Ammiel Hirsch, referenced earlier, argues that Reform policies contributing to congregant alienation from Israel is the truer threat to the Jewish soul. A June 2023 *Jerusalem Post* article entitled "Rabbi Ammiel Hirsch: 'We are losing the soul of the Reform movement,'" adds as a subtitle: "'To turn against Israel is a sign of Jewish illness,' Hirsch said Wednesday." The quotes were from a conference Hirsch organized on "Recharging Reform Judaism." The article cites him as

39 Elliot Jaeger, "Have Reform Jews Given Up on Israel?" *Jerusalem Post*, January 7, 2016.
40 Ibid.

express[ing] his concern that the North American Reform movement is at an inflection point in its history. He said he fears that if the movement becomes perceived as antizionist and anti-particularistic, most American Jews will abandon it, He stated: "If the . . . movement, in word or in deed, by action or by silence, becomes, in fact, or even in perception, an antizionist, anti-particularistic movement that cares only, or mostly, about universal concerns, unanchored in, and unmoored from, the centrality of Jewish peoplehood, most American Jews will abandon us."[41]

Another indication of the gulf between consensus Israeli views and those of Jacobs was his response to President Trump's announcement in December 2017 that he would be moving the American embassy in Israel to Jerusalem. It should be noted that the announcement made clear the embassy would be in pre-1967 Israeli Jerusalem and its move therefore would not pre-judge the resolution of borders, which would have to be decided in bilateral negotiations between the Israelis and the Palestinians. Nevertheless, Jacobs quickly issued a statement on behalf of the Union for Reform Judaism that, among other points, declared, "[W]e cannot support his decision to begin preparing that move now, absent a comprehensive plan for a peace process."[42]

Israelis almost universally supported the embassy move,[43] and the Palestinian leadership has repeatedly demonstrated its lack of interest in genuine peace, but Jacobs somehow construes the Jewish soul as requiring that the Palestinians be given a veto over America's moving its Israeli embassy to Israel's capital. In the same statement, Jacobs further declared that, "Additionally, any relocation of the American Embassy to West Jerusalem should be conceived and executed in the broader context reflecting Jerusalem's status as a city holy to Jews, Christians and Muslims alike."[44] But how could

---

41 Zvika Klein, "Rabbi Ammiel Hirsch: 'We are losing the soul of the Reform movement,'" *Jerusalem Post*, June 1, 2023.

42 "Reform Jewish Movement: Concerned about White House Jerusalem Announcement," Union for Reform Judaism, December 5, 2017.

43 See, for example, Shibley Telhami, "Poll: Jewish Israelis Love Trump," Brookings Institute, May 15, 2018, https://www.brookings.edu/articles/poll-jewish-israelis-love-trump/; "Poll Shows Deep Division between Israeli and US Jews on Trump, Peace, Religion," *Times of Israel*, June 10, 2018, https://www.timesofisrael.com/poll-shows-deep-divisions-between-israeli-and-us-jews-on-trump-peace/.

44 "Reform Jewish Movement: Concerned."

the embassy move reflect negatively on the city's religious status, especially given that it has only been under Israeli governance that the city's significance to all three monotheistic religions has been respected? In his response to the proposed embassy move, Jacobs demonstrated his indifference to Israeli opinion and his sensitivity to the views of Israel's critics on the American Left. In this instance, while he may have had the backing of others in the Reform leadership, there were many in the rank and file who opposed his stance.

Indeed, there were significant, or at least vocal, segments of the Reform movement that opposed the selection of Jacobs as president of the URJ in 2011 because of his affiliations with groups in many respects hostile to Israel. Jacobs at the time was a member of the rabbinic cabinet of J Street and on the board of the New Israel Fund. J Street characterizes itself as pro-Israel and pro-peace, but its pro-Israel claims are belied by its stances.

Israelis of almost all political stripes reject a return to the pre-1967 armistice lines, the so-called Green Line, in any Israeli-Palestinian agreement.[45] The consensus is, as the authors of UN Security Council Resolution 242—the key UN document relating to the territorial issue—asserted, that those lines left Israel too vulnerable and invited further aggression against the country.[46]

Yitzhak Rabin, in his last Knesset speech prior to his assassination, listed West Bank areas—an incomplete list, as he indicated—that Israel would need to retain and populate in any final settlement to assure its security and survival. Yet J Street opposes any Israeli presence beyond the Green Line and advocates the United States supporting, via unilateral policy initiatives, a UN Security Council resolution, or an initiative in conjunction with other major powers, the reversal of Resolution 242 and endorsement of the Green Line as the basis for defining a future border.[47]

---

45 "Security Council Resolution 242 according to Its Drafters," CAMERA, January 15, 2007, https://www.camera.org/article/security-council-resolution-242-according-to-its-drafters/.

46 "Poll: 77% of Israelis Oppose Going Back to the Pre-'67 Lines," *Jerusalem Post*, June 6, 2011, https://www.jpost.com/Diplomacy-and-Politics/Poll-77-percent-of-Israelis-oppose-going-back-to-pre-67-lines.

47 See, for example, "Our Policy" statement on "Occupation, Annexation and Settlements," JStreet, https://jstreet.org/settlements/; "J Street Calls for Stronger American Response to Israeli Settlement Expansion," press release, JStreet, June 6, 2014, https://jstreet.org/press-releases/j-street-calls-for-stronger-american-response-to-israeli-settlement-expansion_1/; "Without Strong Action, Israeli Government Will Continue to Ignore US Opposition to Settlement Expansion," press release, JStreet, October 6, 2016, https://jstreet.org/press-releases/

J Street also advocates the United States instituting punitive measures against Israel for any activity beyond the Green Line. It claims that a number of American administrations have viewed settlements beyond the Green Line as "illegal," when in fact only the Carter administration labeled them illegal and, as attested to by many experts in the field, there is much in international law that weighs in favor of their legality.[48]

Prior to the October 7, 2023, massacre, Israelis had fought four wars against Hamas in thirteen years. Each conflict was triggered by Hamas attacks, particularly rocket fire, against Israel's civilian population. Yet J Street has repeatedly drawn a moral equivalence between Israel and its openly genocidal foe, and has often parroted Hamas claims and statistics about the course of the conflicts and the resultant casualties.[49]

J Street is consistently silent about the goals of Hamas and of the Palestinian Authority and their mutual rejection of the legitimacy of a Jewish state within any borders in "Palestine." It does not address the PA's rejection of all negotiation proposals offered by Israel or by the United States.

J Street asserts it opposes the "global BDS movement" that targets all of Israel for boycott, divestment, and sanction, but does not oppose BDS efforts targeting the territories beyond the Green Line. It sees such boycotts as consistent with its goal of promoting Israeli withdrawal to the Green Line. But, again, the vast majority of Israelis, along with notable Western military and strategic experts, believe such a withdrawal would render Israel fatally vulnerable.[50]

In addition, the "global BDS movement" also sometimes promotes, like J Street, more circumscribed boycotts limited to the "territories," as in its partially successful efforts to advance such boycotts in Europe. It does so because it knows that even such limited boycotts, which serve to weaken Israel's presence in the territories and to advance the goal of Israeli retreat to the Green Line, also serve to undermine Israel's strategic viability and ultimate survival.

---

without-strong-action-israeli-government-will-continue-ignore-us-opposition-settlement-expansion/; "The Settlements are Illegal. It's Past Time to Say So," petition, JStreet, https://act.jstreet.org/sign/the_i_word.

48 Ibid.

49 See, for example, "Statement by Jeremy Ben-Ami, Executive Director, on Israeli Airstrikes in Gaza," press release, JStreet, December 27, 2008, https://jstreet.org/press-releases/statement-jeremy-ben-ami-executive-director-israeli-airstrikes-gaza/.
     Chris Gold, "J Street Spars with Reform Judaism Leader over Gaza," Hill, January 5, 2009.

50 See, for example, "Our Policy" statement on "Boycott, Divestment and Sanctions (BDS)," JStreet, https://jstreet.org/boycott-divestment-and-sanctions-bds/.

J Street has worked with supporters of the Iranian government and strongly backed President Obama's 2015 agreement with Iran that legitimized that nation's nuclear program and released to the mullahs over $100 billion in embargoed funds in exchange for limited curtailment of its pursuit of operable nuclear weapons. It did so even as Iran has consistently reasserted its goal of annihilating Israel and used its resources to arm and finance terrorist proxies, such as Hamas and Hezbollah, that target Israel. Of course, Israelis of virtually all political stripes opposed the Iran agreement.[51]

Shortly before the consummation of the Obama administration's Iran deal, at J Street's annual conference in March 2015, J Street Board of Advisors member Marcia Freedman, echoing those in the last century who opposed a Jewish state even as Jews were being subjected to mass slaughter for lack of a sanctuary, declared that Jews should become a minority in an Arab-dominated binational state.[52] Her suggestion was apparently greeted with much display of assent by fellow panelists and her audience. She and they seem to have no difficulty depriving Jews of the right of national self-determination accorded other peoples. Nor were they troubled by the horrific treatment widely meted out to religious and ethnic minorities, such as Christians, Yazidis, and Kurds as well as Jews, in the Arab world; meted out even more dramatically in the context of events that marked the "Arab Spring" from its inception in 2011.

Jews becoming a minority in a binational state is not official J Street policy. But the leadership of J Street is obviously less interested in the concerns shared by most Israelis, the realities of their predicament, and the well-being of the Jewish state than in aligning itself with elements of the American Left indifferent at best towards those concerns and realities and Israel's fate.

J Street's stances in the wake of the October 7 massacre have been of a piece with its earlier positions. Among Israelis, the focus immediately after the attack and in the following months was on mourning the dead, recovering the hostages, pursuing a campaign in Gaza that would end Hamas's military and political control and prevent its promised unleashing of additional massacres, and preventing and responding to attacks from Hezbollah, from the Houthis of Yemen, and from terror cells in Judea and Samaria, Syria, and Iraq. J Street's focus was elsewhere. Its overarching emphasis was on pushing for an end to

---

51 "Our Policy" statement on "Iran," JStreet, https://jstreet.org/iran/; "J Street Received over $500,000 to Push Iran Deal," *Times of Israel*, May 22, 2016.

52 Elder of Zion, "J-Street Speaker Calls for Calls for Destruction of Israel— to Applause," *Algemeiner*, March 27, 2015, https://www.algemeiner.com/2015/03/27/j-street-speaker-calls-for-destruction-of-israel-to-applause-video/.

hostilities and implementation of a "peace plan" that would yield a Palestinian state in Gaza and the West Bank. Its most definitive policy recommendations, as reflected in its "Issue Briefs"[53] in the months following the massacre, included expediting American recognition of a Palestinian state and rejection of any proposed sanctioning of the International Criminal Court in response to its issuing of arrest warrants against Prime Minister Netanyahu and former Israeli defense minister Yoav Gallant.

As noted, in addition to being a member of J Street's rabbinic cabinet at the time of his appointment to the presidency of the URJ, Jacobs was also on the board of the New Israel Fund (NIF). The NIF is an umbrella organization that finances a number of Israeli NGOs, many of which are likewise hostile to the views and concerns of the vast majority of Israelis. Some NIF grant recipients challenge the right of Jews to national self-determination.[54]

In the wake of the post-October 7, 2023, anti-Israel and often openly anti-semitic demonstrations on the nation's campuses and the targeting of Jewish students for verbal attack and intimidation, and at times physical assault, Jacobs wrote an end-of-academic-year letter, referenced earlier. It is dated May 15, 2024, and headed "Dear Reform College Students." Jacobs reports in the letter,

> A few weeks ago, I went up to Columbia to experience the protests directly. I heard disparate voices. On the one hand, I heard some of the same hateful, vile antisemitic taunts from non-student agitators that strongly supported Hamas' rhetoric calling for the elimination of Israel and harming Jews wherever we live.
>
> I also heard students from the encampment protesting the enormous toll the war in Gaza is exacting on innocent Gazan civilians. Their protest most closely resembled a 1960s non-violent civil rights or peace protest. Freedom of speech is an essential right, while incitement to violence is not.

Jacobs gives no indication of how he determined that the hateful messages he heard were the work of outside agitators and why he associates protesting students only with messages "[resembling] a 1960s non-violent civil rights

---

53   "Issues Briefs," #19, March, 2024, and #24, May 2024, JStreet, https://jstreet.org/j-street-policy-center-issue-briefs-and-memos/.
54   See, for example, "New Israel Fund," NGO Monitor, June 21, 2018.

or peace protest." It is doubtful that the many Jewish students subjected to anti-Jewish screeds, taunting, and even assaults on Columbia's campus would agree with his parsing and whitewashing. But it is consistent with, as discussed in Chapter 3, Jacobs's and the Reform Movement's opposition to codifying into law the IHRA definition of antisemitism because of concerns that its references to some attacks on Israel being antisemitic "would trigger potentially problematic punitive action to circumscribe speech, efforts which have been particularly aimed at college students and human rights activists." Jacobs's downplaying of student involvement in the Jew-hatred on display on Columbia's campus, and he and his associates' downplaying of students' and human rights activists' engagement in antisemitic speech and actions as defined in the IHRA definition of antisemitism, are of a piece. They reflect his and his associates' choice to prioritize defending left-leaning constituencies with which they identify over defending their religious constituency against anti-Jewish bigotry.

Much of the subsequent content of Jacobs's letter builds on his benign rendering of the Columbia students' protests, and he urges empathy with their message. Towards the end of the letter, Jacobs writes,

> When you return to campus (or if you remain engaged in addressing the crisis this summer), if you wish to support Israel, we hope you will turn to your Hillel for opportunities and guidance. If you wish to criticize Israel's policies of occupation of the Palestinians, you can do so as a supporter of Israel's democracy and long-term security. If you wish to protest Israel's policies in prosecuting the war in Gaza, we hope you will do so in a manner that affirms Israel's right to exist as a secure, democratic, and Jewish state and not do so in a way that legitimizes calls for an end to Israel's existence.

It is noteworthy that he is non-judgmental as he addresses in an evenhanded manner those students who "wish to support Israel" and those who "wish to criticize" or "protest Israel's policies." And his advice to the former is to work with their campus Hillel, even though Hillel has generally, on most campuses where there has been significant anti-Israel activity in the wake of October 7, 2023, been minimally engaged in responding to the anti-Israel and anti-Jewish onslaught. Jacobs also speaks of the "occupation" as a given, even though there has been no Israeli presence in Gaza since 2005, and, other than responding to terror out of the West Bank, Israel has largely ceded control of the territory to the Palestinian Authority pending—as per the Oslo accords—a bilaterally negotiated disposition of the territory.

There is no urging students to take a pro-Israel stance and actively make Israel's case against antizionist campus forces. Nor is there any suggestion—as he speaks of students who may wish to "protest Israel's policies in prosecuting the war in Gaza"—that the current protests are largely based on distortions of what is actually happening in Gaza and that Jewish students might consider countering those distortions. And he urges those who wish to protest to "not do so in a way that legitimizes calls for an end to Israel's existence." Why would he not say clearly that to do otherwise, to be silent in the face of, or to join in, calls for an end to Israel's existence would be to exhibit a moral bankruptcy that would put the student beyond the pale of what Reform Judaism represents and advocates? The weak messages that permeate Jacobs's letter to Reform students seem more focused on being sensitive to the anti-Israel bias rife among a left-wing constituency with which he identifies than in leading Reform congregants—even in the wake of the atrocities of October 7, 2023, and the antisemitic tsunami that has followed—in actively fighting against today's Jew-hatred.

With regard to Jacobs's embrace of J Street and additional groups that purvey stances hostile to Israel, other leaders of major American Jewish organizations have done likewise. Jonathan Greenblatt, head of the Anti-Defamation League and formerly a special assistant to President Obama, spoke at J Street's 2016 annual convention and echoed some of its habitual drawing of moral equivalences between Israel and those openly dedicated to the Jewish state's annihilation. He also urged extending greater legitimacy to the Palestinian "narrative": the Palestinian denial of any Jewish historical connection to the land of Israel, and the confabulated rewriting of virtually the entire history of the Arab-Israeli conflict.[55]

The ADL under Greenblatt and his predecessor, Abe Foxman, has criticized state and federal efforts to pass anti-BDS legislation, including decisions to withhold funds from institutions of higher learning that enact BDS measures. The ADL has argued that its stance is based on the defense of freedom of speech.[56] But it requires considerable logical contortion to twist into a free

55 "Remarks by Jonathan A. Greenblatt," ADL, April 17, 2016, https://www.adl.org/resources/news/remarks-jonathan-greenblatt.
56 See, for example, Morton A. Klein and Liz Berney, Esq., "Why does the ADL Continue to Hinder Anti-BDS Efforts?," Zionist Organization of America, June 20, 2016, https://zoa.org/2016/06/10327738-why-does-the-adl-continue-to-hinder-anti-bds-efforts/.

speech issue the withholding of taxpayer funds from publicly supported colleges and universities that pursue policies biased against Israel and ultimately aimed at undermining that nation's viability. The ADL stance seems another instance of conforming to the political predilections of particular echelons in America with which its leaders identify, with little regard for the impact on Israelis.

Examples abound of mainstream Jewish entities accommodating even the most extreme manifestations of Jewish hostility to Israel. Illustrative is accommodation of Jewish Voice for Peace (JVP). JVP militates for Israel's dissolution.[57] It is most active on campuses, where it works as, in effect, the Jewish auxiliary of the Arab-dominated Students for Justice in Palestine (SJP) in promoting BDS resolutions and activities and in silencing pro-Israel voices. In the wake of the October 7 massacre, JVP and other similar Jewish groups have played a major role in the anti-Israel protests that have wracked university campuses, city streets, and myriad public venues.[58]

In April 2018, the Durham, North Carolina, city council voted to ban city police "military-style" training with any foreign entities and prohibit police exchanges of any sort with Israel. Israel is the only nation named in the ban. The city council resolution was spearheaded by JVP activists.[59]

According to a Jewish News Service story of May 6, 2018, one of the activists, Sandra Korn, "is a board member and head of adult education at Durham's Judea Reform Congregation" and works as a youth Midrasha teacher at the Jewish Federation of Durham-Chapel Hill. Another, Lara Haft, "is a Hebrew-school teacher at Beth El Synagogue for the Jewish Federation."[60] Leaders of both the Judea Reform Congregation and Beth El Synagogue emphasized that their congregations and communities include people with diverse opinions. Rabbi Daniel Greyber of Beth El stated that his community "offers every Jew a place to study and pray."[61] But for Jewish institutions to employ

---

57 See, for example, "What Is Your Position regarding Palestinian Refugees?" under "Policies," Jewish Voice for Peace, 2016, https://www.jewishvoiceforpeace.org/wp-content/uploads/2014/06/jvp-faq-page-2016.pdf.

58 See, for example, "Who Are the Palestinian and Jewish-Led Groups Leading the Protests against Israel's Action in Gaza?" PBS News, November 16, 2023.

59 Miriam Elman, "Demonization: Durham NC City Council Bans Police Exchanges with Israel," Legal Insurrection, April 22, 2018, https://legalinsurrection.com/2018/04/demonization-durham-nc-city-council-bans-police-exchanges-with-israel/.

60 Eliana Rudee, "Durham BDS Activists Employed by Local Synagogues, Federation," Jewish News Syndicate, May 7, 2018.

61 Ibid.

as teachers and community leaders individuals who aggressively militate for Israel's destruction, who campaign in American colleges and universities and lobby in American political fora to advance that objective, reflects something more than open-mindedness. It is an indication that those institutions place their support for Israel's well-being and survival at a lower priority level than their conforming to current progressivist dogma about diversity, where diversity means giving legitimacy to whatever the radical elements of the Left are promoting, including attacks on Israel aimed at its dissolution.

Another example: Hebrew Union College-Jewish Institute of Religion is the largest Jewish seminary in North America. According to its self-description, it is "the academic, spiritual, and professional leadership development center of Reform Judaism." For its Los Angeles campus graduation ceremony on May 14, 2018, it recruited as its commencement speaker author Michael Chabon, known for his anti-Israel views.

In 2017, Chabon and his wife, Ayelet Waldman, who is also a writer and also has a long history of vilifying Israel, solicited essays from other writers from around the world on the horrors of the Israeli "occupation" and published them along with essays of their own in a book entitled *Kingdom of Olives and Ash: Writers Confront the Occupation.* The various pieces are filled with factual inaccuracies about supposed Israeli misdeeds, but the bigger problem is the overarching false premise: that the current state of affairs, and all its negative impact on the lives of Palestinians, are perpetuated by Israel's heartless desire to maintain the status quo and prevent Palestinians from assuming fuller control over their own lives. There is nothing on the violence that followed upon Israel's ceding much of its control in the context of the Oslo agreements. There is nothing on the Palestinian leadership's rejection of every Israeli offer of a final territorial division, its refusal to propose counter-offers, its insistence that it will never accede to any final resolution that recognizes Israel's right to exist within any borders. There is nothing on the three wars that had—by the time of the book's publication—been triggered by Hamas attacks, wars that followed upon Israel's unilateral withdrawal from Gaza. All that is apparently deemed inconsequential, not worthy of note, in *Kingdom of Olives and Ash.*[62]

Rabbi David Ellenson, in his introduction of Chabon at the HUC-JIR graduation, reportedly referred to his having written a book on "the occupation" and suggested the book was particularly relevant now because of

---

62   Michael Chabon and Ayelet Waldman, eds., *Kingdom of Olives and Ash: Writers Confront the Occupation* (New York: Harper Perennial, 2017).

the decision to relocate the American Embassy in Israel to Jerusalem.[63] In his speech, Chabon picked up on a theme he addressed in his essay in the 2017 collection: He claimed that the security barrier built by Israel during the terror war in reality had nothing to do with security but was intended to "imprison" Palestinians. Other remarks were in the same vein.[64] According to a graduate at the event, Chabon's observations were greeted with wide audience approval and his speech received enthusiastic applause.[65]

A story by the Jewish Telegraphic Agency on the subsequent controversy about the choice of Chabon as commencement speaker noted these responses from heads of the HUC-JIR: "As both an Israeli and American institution, belonging to two proud democracies defined by lively civil discourse, it does not occur to us at HUC-JIR to quash or vilify political criticism of Israel out of a preemptive fear of controversy," wrote Rabbi David Ellenson, the interim president and chancellor emeritus, and Joshua Holo, the dean of the Los Angeles campus of HUC-JIR. "On the contrary, we know that the confidence to invite challenging ideas both defines and validates democracy in the first place."[66]

But, of course, the issue is not one of quashing free speech but of honoring someone who dismisses Israel's legitimate security concerns and blames Israel, rather than those who seek the Jewish state's destruction, for the difficulties of the Palestinians. Once again, a major, mainstream Jewish body placed Israel's well-being second to accommodating the Israel-vilifying rhetoric that is currently so popular within leftist circles.

Hillel and Other Jewish Organizations, American Educational Institutions, and Israel

Hillel's checkered record in recent years is among the most consequential examples of a mainstream Jewish organization accommodating Jewish

---

63 "Special Memorandum: Concerning the Recent HUC Graduation," Coalition for Jewish Values, May 28, 2018, https://coalitionforjewishvalues.org/2018/05/special-memorandum-concerning-the-recent-huc-graduation/.

64 Michael Chabon, "Those People, Over There," *Tablet Magazine*, May 30, 2018. (Text of commencement speech.)

65 Morin Zaray, "Why I Walked Out on My Graduation," *Atlanta Jewish Times*, May 30, 2018.

66 Ben Sales, "Michael Chabon Attacks Jewish Inmarriage and Israel's Occupation in Speech to Rabbinical Students," Jewish Telegraphic Agency, May 25, 2018.

groups hostile to Israel. Hillel has long been the leader in providing Jewish activities and connectedness on campuses to students. It reports that it has a presence at more than 550 colleges and universities. With regard to Israel, Hillel International guidelines declare that it is "steadfastly committed to the support of Israel as a Jewish and democratic state with secure and recognized borders as a member of the family of nations."[67] The guidelines also assert that

> Hillel will not partner with, house, or host organizations, groups, or speakers that as a matter of policy or practice: Deny the right of Israel to exist as a Jewish and democratic state with secure and recognized borders; delegitimize, demonize, or apply a double standard to Israel; support boycott of, divestment from, or sanctions against the State of Israel; [or] exhibit a pattern of disruptive behavior towards campus events or guest speakers or foster an atmosphere of incivility.[68]

But in recent years students on some campuses have taken exception to these guidelines and insisted, for example, that their campus Hillels host events co-sponsored by the virulently anti-Israel and often openly antisemitic Students for Justice in Palestine and the hardly less anti-Israel Jewish Voice for Peace. Under the rubric "Open Hillel," advocates of this course claim they are simply seeking to broaden the discussion of Israel beyond the positions articulated in the Hillel guidelines.

The first "Open Hillel" conference was held in the fall of 2014 and reportedly drew more than 350 participants. Jewish Voice for Peace played a prominent role in the conference program, as did other voices hostile to Israel and militating against its very existence. An attendee, writing in the *Tower* magazine, noted that, "while there were definitely some views expressed that were even more extreme than JVP, I never heard a single opinion expressed that could be called more ardently Zionist than J Street—which itself has a very problematic relationship with Zionism."[69]

Currently, it is not unusual for Hillel chapters to partner with organizations that support BDS at some level and promote other anti-Israel

67 "Israel," Hillel, https://www.hillel.org/israel-guidelines/.
68 "Standards of Partnership," Hillel, https://www.hillel.org/israel-guidelines/.
69 Aiden Pink, "'Open Hillel' Is a Much Bigger Problem Than You Think," *Tower* 20 (November 2014), https://www.thetower.org/article/open-hillel-is-a-much-bigger-problem-than-you-think/.

policies—most notably J Street, but also at times groups such as JVP and even SJP. A key explanation for this is that, while many Hillel directors are fully supportive of Hillel International's guidelines regarding Israel and are unabashed supporters of the Jewish state and its right to demand a genuine and defensible peace in return for concessions, many other Hillel directors are not. Whether because of views they held before coming to their Hillel positions or because they have been won over to popular campus biases, they are sympathetic to the intellectually insupportable and morally obtuse blaming of Israeli policy for the absence of peace and for the wide hostility to Israel in academic circles.

Moreover, Hillel International has not aggressively sought to hold Hillel chapters to the organization's guidelines on Israel as a condition for their continuing to use the Hillel name. Nor has the wider community of leading Jewish organizations openly addressed the highly problematic developments within this key Jewish campus institution, much less taken a stance on those developments. No doubt this is, again, in large part because so many prominent figures in those organizations are not prepared to challenge the various Israel-baiting segments of society, such as major elements of academia, with which they identify. They prefer instead to blame Israeli policy for those groups' hostility to Israel.

Some voices in Jewish leadership are essentially sympathetic to the strong Hillel International parameters regarding Israel but at the same time argue that Jewish organizational life ought to provide a "big tent" and be open to Jews of all opinions who want to identify with the community. Proponents of this view suggest, regarding Hillel, that it should be seen as a net positive if those Jewish students so critical of Israel nevertheless want to be part of campus Jewish communal life.

But, of course, they want to be part of Hillel not in order to share a common space with Jewish students different from themselves—that is to say, Jewish students who see Israel differently from how they do. If that were their interest, they would create an "Open J Street" and "Open JVP." Rather, they want to be part of Hillel so they can undermine support for Israel from within the flagship Jewish campus organization and use the organization in their quest to separate identifying with Israel—at least Israel as comprehended by and defended by the great majority of Israelis—from Jewish identity.

Compromising defense of Israel in order to "enlarge the tent" by appeasing those who traffic in stances advocated by seekers of the Jewish state's destruction is at once morally reprehensible and likely doomed to failure, if the ultimate objective is to moderate the views of Jewish students hostile to Israel. In November 2017, Rabbi Julie Roth of Princeton's Hillel canceled a talk by Israeli Deputy Foreign Minister Tzipi Hotovely in the wake of protests against Hotovely's appearance by J Street and others.[70] It is highly unlikely that Rabbi Roth did so because she thought her disinviting Hotovely would somehow increase support for Israel from within the circles of Israel's Jewish critics on campus. Did those in Hillel International who tolerated Roth's blackballing of Hotovely believe it would?

In the so-called Al Aqsa Intifada that began in the fall of 2015, the PA urged Palestinians to defend the Al Aqsa mosque from what it falsely claimed to be Israeli depredations. Israelis were soon being killed by Palestinian assailants. A Jewish student group at Stanford wanted to hold a vigil for the Israeli victims and asked the Hillel rabbi, Serena Eisenberg, to lead the memorial prayer. But she reportedly refused to do so because the Palestinian assailants who were killed in the course of their attacks were not also being memorialized and because J Street was not co-sponsoring the event.[71] It is likely that Rabbi Eisenberg was not simply bowing to J Street students and like-minded others but was acting on her own predilections. In any case, does the American Jewish community really want to embrace this new comprehension of Jewish morality? And, if not, how much will the community nevertheless be silent and hamstrung because this is the morality of the day as pushed by the elites with whom it identifies?

On January 21, 2025, as former Israeli prime minister Naftali Bennett was speaking on the second floor of the Joseph Slifka Center for Jewish Life at Yale, Yale's Hillel, students connected with Yalies4Palestine and Jews for a Ceasefire, occupied the first floor. They reportedly chanted anti-Israel slogans, including demands promoting the Hamas-linked BDS campaign for divestment from Israel and calls for Israel's destruction. According to students who witnessed the hostile invasion and were upset by it, those among them who tried to film and record the event were obstructed from doing so, and even told to leave the building, by Slifka Center staff, who were apparently

70 See, for example, Raphael Ahren, "Princeton Hillel Cancels Hotovely Speech after Dovish Jewish groups Protest," *Times of Israel*, November 6, 2017.
71 See, for example, Paul Miller, "Is Jewish Students' Safe Space on Israel Threatened by 'Pro-Israel' Lobby?" *Jewish News Service*, April 2, 2017.

supervising the protest.[72] Did the participation of Jews for a Ceasefire in the protest prompt the Hillel staff to interpret the event as consistent with a "big tent" policy? Is this behavior, clearly in violation of Hillel International's guidelines regarding Israel, really okay with the powers that be at Hillel? And, again, how much will the American Jewish community remain passive in the face of, and even embrace, self-styled pro-peace Jewish groups that promote policies aimed at the destruction of the Jewish state?

Israel's primary obligation is not to win a popularity contest, in the world at large, within the ranks of a hostile Left, or within some Jewish "big tent," many of whose members have priorities inimical to the state's well-being. Rather, its obligation is to protect and defend its citizens, build the state along the same ethical, Jewish, and democratic principles that have been its essential guidelines since its founding, and make its case as best it can to the world, including to the jaundiced elements within Jewish circles. It has no obligation to compromise its vital interests for the sake of advancing its case.

American Jews and their institutions that support Israel in its pursuit of that primary obligation should act accordingly. If, for example, campus Hillels exerted themselves to promote an honest, educational exposition of Israel's case, rather than compromising their doing so in order not to offend other-minded Jewish students, they may find that they win over some of those students, particularly among the ambivalent. They will certainly strengthen the resolve of those students genuinely sympathetic to Israel. And as to those who are not winnable, Hillel leaders and others should remember that it has always been thus. Every assault on, and indictment of, Jews has invariably gained the support of some Jews who want to distance themselves from the community of the besieged. And invariably, the Jews who have taken this course have sought to ascribe their doing so to some higher moral purpose. Whenever Jews, or a portion of their community, have been under attack, there has always sprung up the equivalent not only of J Street but of more extreme groups, full-throated supporters of the Jews' attackers, such as Jewish Voice for Peace.

The more comprehensive explication of the history of the Zionist movement, and defense of Israel, that too many Hillels fail to provide is also all too often missing from Jewish education at earlier levels, whether Jewish day schools or after-school programs. It is common for such schools to promote

---

72 Douglas Noel Sandoval, "Betrayal of Students at Yale University's Jewish House on Campus," *Jewish News Syndicate*, February 3, 2025.

support for Israel. But they typically do little to educate their students in the nature of the threats faced by Israel since its inception and the goals of its enemies over the years, the objective of the state's eradication advanced by both the Palestinian Authority and Hamas. They do little to explicate the propaganda war, indoctrination of constituents, and incitement as well as physical attacks undertaken by both Palestinian leaderships to advance their annihilationist agenda. This failure to educate more fully—perhaps out of a desire to avoid material that might be deemed controversial by some—leaves students unprepared for bigoted assaults on Israel, and on them as Israel's supporters, that they will all too often encounter in their colleges and universities.

One of the Jewish organizations established in recent years to oppose Israeli policy is the IfNotNow movement, which identifies "ending the occupation" as its goal and seeks to counter American Jewish entities that they perceive as supporting "the occupation."[73] There is nothing in their literature that notes the many times, including in recent decades, when Palestinian leaders walked away from Israeli and American proposals for dividing the land between the Jordan and the Mediterranean into two states. There is no noting that Gaza has been under full Palestinian control since 2005 and that the vast majority of Palestinians on the West Bank live under Palestinian governance. There is no acknowledging that the rulers of Gaza had, even before October 7, 2023, launched thousands of rockets at Israeli civilians, and that they called not only for the murder of all Israelis but the murder of all Jews. Nor is there acknowledgment of the fact that the leader of the Palestinian Authority has repeatedly asserted he will never recognize the legitimacy of a Jewish state within any borders.

A video of IfNotNow members shows them participating in a ceremony that seems modeled on an Alcoholics Anonymous meeting, except that in the latter the speakers take responsibility for their earlier problematic behavior and humbly seek the strength to forego such behavior in the present and future. In contrast, the IfNotNow members characterize themselves as victims of their past—of Jewish educations that lauded Israel and failed to expose them to Israel's alleged transgressions against the Palestinians—and declare that they have broken free of that past and have set out on a righteous quest to make right Israel's wrongs.

---

73 See "Our Principles," IfNotNow Movement, https://www.ifnotnowmovement.org/principles.

Perhaps these individuals' Jewish education actually provided a fuller immersion in the realities of Israel's relations with its Palestinian neighbors and the challenges entailed in the quest for a more comprehensive separation of the two populations, but they were not paying attention. Or perhaps they chose to jettison what they had learned once they were at college and faced a zeitgeist that rewarded perspectives different from those in which they had been educated. But it could also be that their education in Jewish day schools, after-school programs, summer camps entailed promotion of Israel without exposure to the threats posed by the state's neighbors and the difficulties entailed in addressing those threats. Of course, even this third option would not excuse the partisans of IfNotNow from their failure to educate themselves, but it would represent a weakness of Jewish education that needs to be corrected.

The shortcomings of Israel-related education in Jewish day and after-school programs are only a very small part of the problems surrounding education about Israel in pre-college public and private schools. The larger difficulties, while not caused by Jewish communal organizations, have been allowed to metastasize with Jewish communal organizations and their leadership failing to counter them and at times even blocking efforts to counter anti-Israel bias in the schools.

Texts and curricula produced by Arab states and by academic Middle East Studies departments hostile to Israel have widely been offered to, and adopted by, public and private schools for use in history, social studies, and related courses.[74] Teachers also commonly and uncritically download material from media websites likewise hostile to Israel, with little or no vetting for accuracy or objectivity. Again, Jewish organizations have done little to counter this trend.

An illustrative example is provided by the schools in my own city, the Boston suburb of Newton, Massachusetts, whose population is about one third Jewish. A parent complaint in 2012 about factually false anti-Israel assertions taught in a high school classroom was dismissed by school officials. This led to some grassroots rallying around the issue and to calls for a review of curricula and vetting of anti-Israel bias. School officials responded by stonewalling, rejecting all complaints, and refusing to provide town residents

---

74 See, for example, Jewish Telegraph Agency staff, "Tainted Teachings, What Your Kids are Learning about Israel, America and Islam, Parts 1 through 4," Campus Watch, Middle East Forum, October 27, 2005, https://www.meforum.org/campus-watch/tainted-teachings-what-your-kids-are-learning.

with copies of the curriculum in question—despite Massachusetts state law mandating public access to public school curricula. Rather than support the concerned parents, seek clarification of the curricula, and address the potential problems, the Boston Combined Jewish Philanthropies, Anti-Defamation League, Jewish Community Relations Council, and a number of local rabbis—apparently without examining the relevant teaching materials—all came to the defense of school officials.

Some in the community ultimately turned to Judicial Watch, which filed a Freedom of Information Act (FOIA) petition with the Newton school system, requesting the teaching materials that the system had until then refused to provide. Newton subsequently did hand over relevant course material—how comprehensively is uncertain—beginning in the spring of 2015. Judicial Watch, at the request of community activists, transferred the material for analysis to the Committee for Accuracy in Middle East Reporting and Analysis (CAMERA). (In the interests of full disclosure, I was then a member of CAMERA's national board.) In 2017, CAMERA published a monograph on the material entitled "Indoctrinating Our Youth: How a U.S. Public School Curriculum Skews the Arab-Israeli Conflict and Islam."[75]

Parents' complaints, and the provided material, also touched—in addition to the teaching about Israel—on the teaching of Islam in the schools. Complaints about such teaching have been raised across the nation. They have challenged both the accuracy of what is taught and the appropriateness of teaching Islamic doctrine to an extent that no other religion—most notably Christianity or Judaism—is covered, which would seem to run counter to standard understandings, vis-à-vis public schools, regarding the separation of church and state.

The CAMERA monograph documents myriad factual errors in the course material provided by the Newton school system, as well as omission of information vital to an understanding of the Arab-Israeli conflict, with both the factual errors and the omissions reflecting an anti-Israel bias. The appearance of the monograph finally led the school system to acknowledge publicly a problem with the curricula and to promise reform (although in subsequent statements some school officials backtracked from this straightforward acknowledgment). It also led some of the Jewish leadership that

---

75 Steven Stotsky, *Indoctrinating Our Youth: How a U.S. Public School Curriculum Skews the Arab-Israeli Conflict and Islam* (Boston, MA: Committee for Accuracy in Middle East Reporting in America, 2017).

had uncritically supported the school system but had already somewhat shifted their stances as more information about what was being taught in the schools was revealed—including leadership of the local ADL and JCRC—to acknowledge more fully that there were indeed problems at the schools.

But not everyone among the community's Jewish leaders responded this way. In November 2017, the local Newton newspaper, the *Newton Tab*, published an interview with CAMERA's executive director about the monograph. Included in the interview was a discussion of CAMERA's three recommendations to the Newton Public Schools. These were: 1) having teaching materials carefully vetted for accuracy and academic rigor, 2) making the curriculum and teaching materials easily available to parents and other interested citizens, and 3) excluding from the classroom those materials that had already been proven to be biased and factually unreliable.[76]

A subsequent letter to the *Tab* from five local rabbis, including Toba Spitzer, president of the Massachusetts Board of Rabbis, attacked the article and the monograph. The rabbis declared:

> We are troubled that outside groups [in fact, CAMERA is based in Newton and a number of its board and staff have family members attending Newton public schools] with a clear political agenda are trying to advance their own interests by criticizing the school system unfairly and inaccurately.
>
> Our ultimate hope is that students in the Newton public schools will learn the stories from both sides of the conflict, and will grow to appreciate that the Israeli-Palestinian conflict is complex, not that one side is "right" and the other "wrong."
>
> That possibility grows smaller when outside parties, including so-called "media watch groups," attempt to dictate what the "truth" is, which group's grievances get aired over the other's, or what curriculum materials should be taught in schools, with the goal of forwarding their own specific agenda.
>
> Just as a variety of opinions about the Israeli-Palestinian conflict exist within the Greater Boston Jewish community about Israel [*sic*], so, too, are there many legitimate angles from which to teach our students about the Israeli-Palestinian conflict.

---

76 Andy Levin, "CAMERA Focuses on Newton Schools' Arab-Israeli Conflict Curriculum," *Newton Tab*, November 21, 2017.

We support the Newton Schools for approaching the subject carefully and with respect for the many human narratives of Israelis and Palestinians, an educational perspective which advances the cause of peace for Israel and her neighbors.[77]

Perhaps not surprisingly, the rabbis did not cite or challenge any of the CAMERA monograph's specific claims of inaccuracies and distortions in the classroom materials handed over by the Newton Schools. There is, in fact, nothing to suggest that any of them actually read the monograph. That rabbis dismiss calls for factual accuracy, and concerns over the many examples of falsehoods taught in the curriculum materials, as a promotion of pro-Israel bias; that they argue, in effect, that there are no facts and no "truth" but only "many human narratives"; and that they declare the objective of the Newton schools should not be teaching about the Israeli-Palestinian conflict as fully and accurately as possible but rather providing what to their particular lights is a "perspective which advances the cause of peace" is another clear example of Jewish community leaders seeking to accommodate popular, primarily leftist, indictments of Israel, however divorced from historical and present reality, and justifying their doing so with claims of being motivated by higher moral purpose.

Anti-Israel curricula and programs have infiltrated public and private schools across America with little if any pushback from Jewish communities and all too often with Jewish support. The assault on Israel at all levels of the American education system will almost inevitably have an impact on American public opinion and ultimately, as its sponsors hope, on American policy. The supine Jewish response will have consequences.

But many American Jews are clearly willing to subsume to other, conflicting, priorities whatever commitment they may feel to Israel's survival and well-being. Many may choose to delude themselves into believing those other priorities and Israel's well-being are in fact reconcilable, or they may simply choose to give precedence to the views of groups with which they identify and which adopt a jaundiced, even hostile, attitude towards Israel. In any case, their falling in line with Israel's often clearly bigoted critics is, again, consonant with recurrent Jewish responses to the circumstance of Jews being under siege. And, once more consonant with historical precedent, those who adopt such attitudes cast their stance as the more ethical course.

---

77 "Letters," *Newton Tab*, December 6, 2017.

A cynic may view it as simply the more self-protective course. But then one can question how self-protective it will ultimately be. The groups with which those who adopt this path identify—generally associated with the so-called "progressive" wing of the American Left—are moving further and further into embracing political positions traditionally inimical to Jews and increasingly tolerating within their ranks not only the open expression of anti-Israel bigotry but of anti-Jewish sentiments as well.

What will the Jewish response be as the Jew-baiting in America, and not merely the anti-Israel bias, becomes more and more explicit? Recent events—as well as the modern history of elements of Jewish communities in Europe and in America seeking to accommodate anti-Jewish sentiment and anti-Jewish indictments, a history that at its inception included, for some, embracing antizionism—may point to how segments of the Jewish community will manage the burgeoning Jew-baiting of the "progressive" Left and the broader Red-Green-Black alliance. Michael Chabon, in his speech at the HUC-JIR commencement, not only reprised his oft-repeated attacks on Israel but also attacked Judaism and essentially advocated the disappearance of the Jewish faith and its followers. He did so in the language of universalism and breaking down barriers.[78] Perhaps the doyens of the "academic, spiritual, and professional leadership development center of Reform Judaism," who so vigorously defended their invitation to Chabon, wanted to impart to their newly minted rabbis and cantors Chabon's answer to the challenges facing the Jewish world. Perhaps they wanted their graduates to consider seriously not only Chabon's anti-Israel arguments but his anti-Jewish proposals as well, his calls for the dissolution of the faith and its followers. Such a course, and not simply a distancing from Israel, is, after all, the logical ultimate step, the *reductio ad absurdum*, in the Jewish accommodation of anti-Jewish sentiment.

---

78 Chabon, "Those People, Over There." At the very end of his speech, Chabon, perhaps feeling obliged to end on a less anti-Jewish note, called for a Judaism of the future that will "[f]ind room in the Jewish community for all those who want to share in our traditions." But, of course, much of the Judaism of the present does that. And to do so is, in fact, to participate in expanding what he devoted most of his speech to attacking and characterizing as requiring dissolution: a "ghetto" in his terms, a community separated from others by adherence to traditions. To conclude his speech in a manner consistent with the preponderance of his argument, with his admonitions against all of Jewish life's separations and barriers, all its intrinsic and extrinsic divides between it and other cultures and belief systems, would have been to acknowledge he is calling for the dissolution of the Jewish faith and its followers.

Epilogue

Steps Towards Addressing the Failures

"An early build-up of a clear and positive feeling of belongingness to the Jewish group is one of the few effective things that Jewish parents can do for the later happiness of their children."

> Kurt Lewin, German-Jewish psychologist and refugee
> from Nazi Germany, in "Bringing Up the Jewish Child" (1940)

"To counteract fear and make the individual strong to face whatever the future holds, there is nothing so important as a clear and fully accepted belonging to a group whose fate has a positive meaning. A long-range view which includes the past and the future of Jewish life, and links the solution of the minority problem with the problem of the welfare of all human beings is one of these possible sources of strength . . . To build up such feeling of group belongingness . . . should be one of the outstanding policies in Jewish education."

> Kurt Lewin, in "Self-Hatred among Jews" (1941)

What is required of the American Jewish community to overcome its failures in the face of rising antisemitism—the hatemongering directed at American Jews and at Israel and Zionism—particularly that coming from the Left, from Islamist/Palestinian sources, and from Black radical sources? These three fonts of antisemitism, while gleaning far less attention from major Jewish organizations than the antisemitism of white supremacists and neo-Nazis, have penetrated much more into the American mainstream (even as they often share antisemitic memes and tropes with white supremacists and neo-Nazis). This is reflected in their virtually ubiquitous presence on the nation's campuses, in their growing influence in grade schools, and in their many followers and mouthpieces in, for example, the halls of Congress, the media, and cultural circles.

The Role of Children's Upbringing in Countering Anti-Jewish Depredations

The citations above from Kurt Lewin about the importance of nurturing in the Jewish child a strong sense of Jewish group belonging may seem only tangentially related to the issue of reversing the stark inadequacy of communal response to the threats confronting American Jews. But members of a besieged minority subjected to hate must be able to resist the wishful, delusional impulse to find some merit in the indictments—however bigoted and absurd they may be. They must resist the fantasy that by doing so and by reforming to address the indictments, or urging reform on other members of the community, they will appease the besiegers. They must resist emulating the abused child who responds to his situation by seeing himself as "bad" and by trying to become "good." Rather, it is only by openly acknowledging the ugliness and depravity of the assaults, whatever their sources, and choosing to call them out and fight them with all its strength, does a community under attack have any hope of defanging the threat.

In the case of abused children, some are fortunate enough to have a consistently nurturing adult in their life, a grandparent perhaps, who conveys to them a sense of being valued and worthy of better treatment despite the parental persecution. That adult may not be able to extricate the child from his or her current circumstances, but can often help the child shed his or her ultimately self-defeating response of self-blame, a response that all too often dooms such children in later years to lives of ongoing self-abasement, frustration, and unending misery.

In besieged communities, as noted before, strong communal institutions can play a similar role. They can convey a sense of the community's worth and integrity and instill a conviction of the unfairness of the assaults and the need to resist them. But in the context of the current attacks on American Jewry, there has been a grievous absence of such institutions; and ones that might have played such a role have failed to do so.

But whatever the state of communal institutions, fostering a nurturing sense of belonging to a valuable and admirable community, worthy of being defended against lies and defamation, should begin in childhood and at home. It should begin with what the child is taught at home and in the course of the Jewish education the family provides for him or her outside the home. Ideally, the teaching will convey the spiritual and intellectual legacy of the child's forebears, the core of the child's own spiritual and intellectual inheritance. It will transmit a substantive understanding of Jewish history, Jewish faith, Jewish ethics and comprehension of a moral life, Jewish culture; an understanding of the span of these elements of Jewish life over more than three millennia.

Beyond this, the child should also be introduced to the challenges to his or her sense of self, the denigration of his or her identity, that he or she is likely to encounter in college or even while still in grade school, and should be armed with how to respond. Children, beyond being taught to know their heritage and to value it, should know more specifically the direction of likely attacks and be able to answer them—whether those attacks target them as American Jews or as Zionists.

Such preparation in childhood is, of course, not a panacea. Some people, despite being well educated, will be temperamentally unprepared to withstand the pressures of anti-Jewish and antizionist assaults. They will seek to flee either spiritually or physically, or both, and will cast their flight as some act of higher morality.

But for most, education will provide a vital bulwark against the psychologically corrosive effects of besiegement. It will enable children, and the adults they become, to derive their morality from something other than the indictments of accusers, to define themselves in terms other than those the haters would impose on them, and to comprehend steadfastly their place in the world as equal to anyone else's, with a claim to the inalienable rights of all people, a claim morally superior to that of the world's haters and bigots.

In recent centuries, the importance of educating Jews in Jewish faith and ethics, Jewish history, and Jewish culture as a defense against the psychological corrosiveness of anti-Jewish depredations, an importance which should have been obvious, has had to be restated, and in effect rediscovered, many times. For example, in the dark days of the Nazi era, as Jews were subjected to new levels of demonization in much of "civilized" Europe and denigrated elsewhere in the world as well, the psychologist Kurt Lewin, himself a refugee from Germany, felt it necessary to point out the importance of teaching children a positive Jewish group identity as a defense against the soul-withering depredations of anti-Jewish hatred. The quotations from his essays, taken as epigraphs for this chapter, illustrate his effort.

Jewish Groups Confronting the Antisemitic Onslaught, and Those Failing to Do So

Returning to the failure of American Jewish communal institutions to play the role required of them in fighting the rising antisemitism of recent years: The community is riven with organizations and leaders that refuse to acknowledge fully the threat posed by the antisemitic hatemongering of groups other than those of the Far Right. While there has been some awakening in response to the October 7 massacre and the torrent of Jew-hatred that has followed, the response is still inadequate. Realistic assessment of the threat, and effective steps to address it, are still undercut by the predilection to downplay the dangers emanating from leftist sources and their allies and also to construe the antisemitic assault from sources other than the Far Right as secondary to hatred of Israel and even as reparable by reform of Israeli policies.

This formulation is a gross betrayal of Israel and of the great majority of American Jews supportive of the Jewish state. It is also a betrayal of the American Jewish community as a whole in that it instills in the community a skewed comprehension of the dangers it faces and thereby renders it even more vulnerable. Those who see a relatively benign Left and a misguided Israel may not rise in their moral turpitude to that of extremist "Jewish" groups such as Jewish Voice for Peace and IfNotNow, which, in their hostility to Israel, make common cause with genocidally antisemitic leftist and Islamist/Palestinian entities. But, in contorting themselves to curb their criticism of anti-Israel bodies not affiliated with the Far Right, those Jewish organizations and leaders who ply the "blame Israel" course essentially give a pass to such bodies, whether drawn from academia, the Democrat Party, the so-called "liberal" churches, Islamist-dominated Muslim groups, or Black radical groups, and to their antisemitic agendas.

The dramatic increase in American antisemitism in recent years should have made clear, as explicated in Chapter Three, that much of the Jewish organizational response has been strategically and morally bankrupt in its distancing from Israel. In addition, it has been strategically and morally blind to the reality that the American Jewish community is not simply the incidental victim of hostility to Israel. Rather, it is at least as much the target of the murderous hatred as is the Jewish state. Yet major elements of the community, and seemingly most of its mainstream leadership, remain blind to this reality. They don't want to believe it, they don't want to rethink old, comforting delusions, and so they close their eyes. It is as though the canary in the mine had the wherewithal to counter the rising toxic fumes, or at least to attempt to counter them, but refused to act.

History is full of besieged communities deluding themselves about their circumstances, seeking to ingratiate themselves with their besiegers, and thereby exacerbating their tragedies and suffering additional losses upon losses. If that denouement is to be avoided by the American Jewish community, and by an undermined Jewish nation whose well-being many in the community—although still a minority—and in its leadership seem so willing to compromise, then the community requires a major rethinking. It also needs to empower a very different leadership, one which will fight antisemitism in all its forms, proudly and unabashedly, as Jews and as Americans. But how do we get from here to there?

Among the failing Jewish organizations and leaderships, the most significant are old, well-established institutions such as the Anti-Defamation League, International Hillel, numerous federations, JCRCs and their umbrella body, various seminaries and rabbinical groups, and many mainstream congregations. Their establishment heft renders their failures all the more damaging.

In contrast, those fighting back against the antisemitism and antizionism of the Left, of Islamist/Palestinian groups, of Black radicals and their intersectional allies are typically smaller activist Jewish groups. They have challenged such purveyors of anti-Jewish hate in their bastions in academia, in the media, in the political arena, in the "liberal" churches, and elsewhere. Some examples of those smaller activist entities and their areas of focus are given below.

CAMERA (Committee for Accuracy in Middle East Reporting and Analysis) has monitored media coverage of Israel and the Israeli-Palestinian and broader Israeli-anti-Israel conflict for more than four decades. It is the leading organization doing so. It also monitors social media and specialty outlets such as scientific journals, school texts, and religious publications. It interacts with editors and reporters to elicit corrections and stop the repetition of false anti-Israel claims. In addition, it publishes critiques of the media to amplify public awareness of flawed reporting and to challenge the media when corrections are not forthcoming or when falsehoods are so egregious as to warrant greater attention. Honest Reporting also monitors some media outlets and has helped raise public awareness of media problems.

In addition to its media work, CAMERA has a program, staffed primarily by former grade school educators, dedicated to fighting DEI- and Islamist-related anti-Israel and anti-Jewish activity in K-12 education. CAMERA has also developed a school curriculum on Jewish history and the Jewish presence in the Land of Israel.

The AMCHA Initiative has been at the forefront of monitoring levels of antisemitic campus activity. It has done pioneering work in demonstrating the correlation between, on the one hand, faculty engagement in pro-BDS and related anti-Israel activity at colleges and universities and, on the other, the level of antisemitic assault to which Jewish students at colleges and universities are subjected. AMCHA Initiative has also played a leading role in exposing antisemitic and anti-Israel material in K-12 curricula in the guise of DEI programs.

The Louis D. Brandeis Center for Human Rights under Law has figured prominently in taking legal action against universities and colleges that tolerate and abet antisemitic and antizionist campus activity. The Deborah Project has provided pro bono legal services to Jews facing discrimination in grade schools and in institutions of higher learning. The Lawfare Project and Shurat HaDin have also pursued legal measures against entities and institutions promoting Jew-hatred, including educational institutions.

The Academic Engagement Network works with university and college faculty and staff seeking to fight anti-Jewish and anti-Israel bigotry on their campuses. StopAntisemitism works, particularly on social media, to expose and counter antisemitic voices and activities emanating from whatever source, including those from campuses.

Club Z is an organization focused on educating Jewish high school students about Jewish and Israeli history and equipping them to address antizionist and antisemitic challenges they may face both while in high school and later in college and in their post-college life. Endowment for Middle East Truth (EMET) is a Washington-based pro-Israel organization focused largely on providing accurate information about Israel to members of Congress.

While historically a number of organizations have had a presence on campus giving direct support to students who seek to promote pro-Israel sentiment and counter anti-Jewish and antizionist campus activists, their presence has diminished in recent years despite the ever-increasing need. Some organizations, such as the Israel Project and the David Project, have simply folded. Others, like Stand with Us and Israel on Campus Coalition, have largely merged their campus activities with Hillel. Consequently, their influence—positive, inconsequential, or negative—on confronting anti-Jewish challenges has become essentially indistinguishable from Hillel's on any particular campus.

Chabad on Campus is present at nearly a thousand colleges and universities worldwide, mainly in the United States. While campus Chabad centers do not engage directly in political activity, many students who are motivated to become involved in pro-Israel activity find their campus Chabad more supportive than the Hillel at their school.

CAMERA has had an independent presence fighting the information war on campuses, supporting both individual pro-Israel activists and campus groups, for more than three decades. It is currently working on about one hundred campuses. Other organizations with an independent campus presence include Students Supporting Israel and End Jew Hatred.

(CAMERA, cited above for its various long-established and effective programs in defense of Israel and the American Jewish community, has recently undergone a Board of Directors-initiated change in leadership and direction which may compromise its activities and raises questions about the future of its programs.)

The above examples are, of course, only a partial list of smaller organizations that have taken on the purveyors of anti-Jewish and anti-Israel bigotry. Their efforts are often supplemented by ad hoc groups such as alumni responding to particular outrages at their alma maters.

These smaller bodies have had many successes in addressing some school and campus problems, episodes of hatemongering by politicians, media distortions and social media Jew-baiting. (Mainstream media and social media outlets typically abet antisemitism promoted by the Left and by Black radicals and Islamist/Palestinian groups both by refusing to challenge it and by giving positive coverage to its purveyors.) In addition, these smaller entities have often been able to work with sympathetic groups from within the communities of the hostile, antisemitic organizations—with African Americans, Muslims, and leftists who are liberals in the traditional sense—to help counter the hatred emanating from those communities.

The achievements of these smaller Jewish groups could be expanded if they had greater resources. Anyone concerned about the rising antisemitism and wishing to counter it should seek these groups out and support them.

The efforts of these groups are, however, often undercut by the large, older Jewish organizations that not only abet the haters by their silence but also, as noted in earlier chapters, at times actually voice support for the haters. The terrible consequences of the absence of major Jewish bodies from the struggle against much of today's antisemitism are indirectly illustrated by the fact that the impact of public confrontation with antisemitism is very different in those exceptional cases when major organizations have been engaged in pushing back along with smaller groups. An example is the community's response and its effect when myriad Jewish groups of all sorts, as well as non-Jewish bodies such as arms of law enforcement, were targeted for "dismantling" by the BDS-linked Boston Mapping Project. Jewish organizations responded almost with one voice, attacking the Project's blatant antisemitism and its threats. Their reaction elicited broad condemnation of the Project by a wide array of figures from across the political spectrum and many public and private groups beyond the Jewish community. Additionally, it prompted FBI involvement in the matter, a bipartisan Congressional letter calling for "significant federal action" regarding the threats posed by the Project, and a splintering of the BDS movement over the issue.

The more common phenomenon is that many mainstream Jewish organizations offer tepid responses or none at all to non-Far Right antisemitism, or even excuse antisemitism from non-Far Right quarters. Not surprisingly, this assures that more such Jew-hatred will come from those quarters. A major factor contributing to the rising antisemitism in America is that it is largely cost-free for its purveyors, who suffer very few negative consequences. Unencumbered by pushback from major Jewish bodies, they are free to reap political gains by pandering to anti-Jewish and anti-Israel constituencies within Far Left, progressive circles, Black radical groups, Islamist/Palestinian groups and their intersectional allies.

The reaction of North Carolina Jewish communal bodies to the North Carolina Democrat Party's passage, in June 2022, of two bigoted, defamatory, antisemitic and antizionist resolutions, discussed in Chapter One, is a case in point. The response of the Charlotte Federation and other Jewish groups in the state was low key and shamefully weak. Jewish leaders in the state refused to push for rescinding of the resolutions. A leader of the state's Jewish Democrats organization remarked that to do so would distract from supposedly more weighty Democrat issues. Such craven pandering to Jew-hatred is hardly likely to diminish the state Democrat Party's blatant promotion of antisemitism. Rather, it virtually assures that its antisemitism will thrive and metastasize.[1]

---

1   See Ravitch and Rosenthal, "Jewish Leaders in North Carolina Betray Jewish Interests."

Another way in which the policies of major Jewish bodies exacerbate the threat from today's antisemitism concerns their conveying to the Jewish community a false sense of something being done to address the problems, when they are, in fact, doing much too little. Most American Jews likely believe that the legacy organizations with which they are familiar must be responding to the attacks on the community. Indeed, they probably receive mailings from those organizations claiming they do so. Community members are lulled into complacency and are not aware of those organizations' failures and of the need to seek out and support alternative groups that are, in fact, working to address the threats.

The failure of so many large long-established Jewish organizations to counter the assaults on American Jews from sources other than the antisemitic Far Right is linked, as noted in earlier chapters, to their leaders identifying with the purveyors of those threats and wishing to maintain and cultivate connections with them rather than criticize them, however ugly and dangerous their hatred. Perhaps those organizational leaders do so because they believe that Jewish well-being is dependent on the community immersing itself in an imagined alliance with disadvantaged groups and groups on the political Left, an alliance which they perceive as having transcendent validity. Or perhaps they have transformed what was originally undertaken as a means of protecting the community into an end in itself. Perhaps they have essentially redefined the Jewish vocation as the cultivating of that imagined alliance. In either case, the result is the same: failure in their most vital of all tasks.

Leaders of major Jewish organizations, including communal organizations such as federations, are not elected, or at least not elected by the community at large. Their failures do not lend themselves to being addressed by community-instigated reforms in governance, unless those reforms are initiated by that relatively narrow segment of the community that holds sway in the relevant organizations. Some voices have suggested that the community should create alternative bodies that will duplicate the traditional mandates of the old established organizations and challenge their primacy. These new institutions would be led by people more prepared to fight Jew-hatred from whatever source. But the strength of the established groups lies largely in that, due to their longevity and their long-standing prominence, they garner financial and other support from people who are motivated by a tradition of supporting them and see this support as giving them a status among, and connections with, their peers in the community. These incentives could not be easily duplicated by new bodies created to challenge the older organizations.

A potentially more fruitful way to counter the failing established bodies may be to look to those among their major financial supporters who might be open to considering the threatening ramifications of their failures and take steps to reform their organizations. This would, of course, mean overcoming the inertia of old habits and their social reinforcements.

Major supporters can roughly be divided into three groups. First, there are those who essentially see the world as the leaders of their organizations do. These are individuals whose priority is cultivating their links to the groups generating non-Far Right antisemitism. They are also predisposed to ignoring, downplaying, or rationalizing the hatred coming from those groups, and to maintaining the delusion of a transcendent connection with them around shared objectives. They, obviously, will not be particularly amenable to rethinking their convictions.

Second, some benefactors are more concerned about the threats facing the American Jewish community as well as the threats to Israel, are sensitive to the hatred coming from sources other than the Far Right, but have not been willing to confront the need for a radical reassessment of their organization's priorities. They have been inclined to live with the dissonance between their perceptions of the Jewish community's peril on the one hand and, on the other, their identification with those groups and institutions in the wider society who play a major role in generating and amplifying that peril.

Then there are those who are very committed to the well-being of the Jewish community and of Israel, who want to use their resources to advance both, but who—while typically very successful businesspeople whose success was built in no small part on due diligence regarding their business endeavors—do not exert that same due diligence to ascertain what their philanthropy is buying. They may well be unhappy with what the major organizations they support are doing or failing to do were they to become more knowledgeable about it.

Notably, a number of philanthropists in wider American society have made statements to the effect that giving money is no sacrifice for them because they have plenty of it. What is more consequential and requires more dedication is giving of their time, of which they do not have plenty. They have typically been referring to taking a hands-on role in the managing of their charities, but the same point can be made with regard to the issue of due diligence. Diligence is also relevant regarding support for the smaller activist organizations that are focused on addressing the antisemitism coming from all sources. Supporters of those organizations should make the effort to ascertain how much the programs receiving their dollars in fact advance the causes to which they are ostensibly dedicated, and whether or not those causes might be better served by directing their philanthropy to other groups.

Another area requiring the dedication of Jewish philanthropists' time as well as of their money is the financing of Jewish and Israeli studies departments at universities. Many Jewish philanthropists, eager to advance the academic study of Jewish and Israeli subjects and also to benefit campuses with which they have some connection, seek to underwrite such departments or Jewish and Israeli chairs in established departments. But given the anti-Jewish and anti-Israel predilections of so many universities and colleges and the hostility of so many faculties, those selected for appointment to the endowed departments and chairs are very often chosen for their hostility to both the Jewish community and to Israel.[2] A much more promising course for those interested in directing their dollars to Jewish or Israeli studies is to offer to establish a free-standing institute affiliated with a college or university but with control, including hiring, remaining in the hands of the benefactors and their representatives. This route typically entails more time and effort but is much more likely to advance the benefactors' objectives. A less demanding alternative is to condition funding for a university chair or department on strict adherence to the tenets defined in the bequest, which would preclude diverting the bequest to anti-Jewish or anti-Israel ends. However, this route can present its own difficulties in terms of enforcement.

A fourth group of benefactors of major Jewish organizations are people whose priorities are focused on the well-being of the Jewish community and of Israel and who have, in fact, seen the failure of their organizations to advance that well-being. These people may well have already withdrawn their support and redirected their contributions to groups whose efforts are more consonant with their priorities.

Major financial supporters of problematic legacy organizations from the second and third groups in the list above, and those in the fourth group who have yet to act on their misgivings, may be amenable to questioning their hands-off approach to the present leadership of their organizations. They should be encouraged to push for changes in the policies of their organizations' current leadership regarding threats to the community and to Israel, and to work for the appointment of new leaders who will introduce such revisions.

---

2   For an indication of the anti-Israel bigotry rampant among Jewish studies and Israel studies academics in America, see, for example, Joshua M. Karlip, "The Demise of Jewish Studies in America—and the Rise of Jewish Studies in Israel," *Commentary*, November 2022.

Jewish newspapers and other publications troubled by the shortcomings of the large legacy organizations should directly address their major financial backers and board members, confronting them with their organizations' failure to tackle the threats and with their responsibility to intervene. The problematic leaders should, of course, also be directly challenged. Articulated community discontent may have an impact on them as well, however reluctant they may be to change their predilections and priorities. The Jewish News Syndicate (JNS) has published many pieces calling out major organizations who fail to protect their communities. It should also name and shame their backers, lay leaders, and executives. The relevant articles, as all JNS pieces, would be available for republication by Jewish newspapers and other outlets.

Individuals in the community also have a role to play. They can write to the problematic legacy organizations to express their concerns and criticisms as community members. If they are or have been donors, they should note this as they make their discontent known. Of course, the more they know about an organization's failures, the more informed can their communication be and the more seriously it will be taken.

The role of individuals cannot be overstated. The great majority of American Jews want to protect their community and the America-Israel relationship from all domestic threats, whether emanating from sources Left or Right, Black or White, Islamist or secularist, progressive or regressive. American Jews should familiarize themselves with those threats, with the stances of major Jewish organizations, and with what is going on in those communal institutions with which they have some connection. How much do those institutions seek to call out and confront the haters, whatever the haters' politics and affiliations? How much do they shrink from confrontation and ignore, downplay, or even excuse the hatred from imagined "allies"? What is going on in their synagogues with regard to the rising challenges to the Jewish community and to Zionism? What is being taught in their children's and grandchildren's Hebrew schools and Jewish day schools? (And, for that matter, what is being taught in their public schools about Jews and about Israel?) What about the colleges their children and grandchildren are attending, and their own alma maters; what is being taught there and what role is being played by their campus Hillels? Individuals must inform themselves and act. They must act on their own, or with like-minded friends, or join and support one of those very effective smaller community organizations such as those listed above. The time for detachment and passivity is long past.

Government's Role in Countering the Antisemitic Assault and the Community's Role in Prodding It to Do More

Elected officials and federal and state governments can play a role in fighting the rising antisemitism, and at times have done so. In some instances, they have enforced anti-discrimination laws relevant to antisemitism on campuses, and initiated and implemented state anti-BDS legislation. But they can do much more. For example, they can enforce both anti-discrimination laws and anti-BDS legislation more routinely and aggressively.

In a statement under the heading: "Know Your Rights: Title VI and Religion," the US Department of Education Office for Civil Rights (OCR) has declared that it "enforces federal civil rights laws that prohibit schools, colleges and universities from discriminating based on race, color, national origin, sex, disability or age." While Title VI does not protect students from religious discrimination, the OCR explains that other federal civil rights laws do. In addition, as in the case of antisemitism on campuses, the attacks on Jews are almost invariably attacks on Jewish ethnicity and national origin, and so do fall within the purview of Title VI. The OCR can be much more aggressive in fighting the antisemitism metastasizing across the nation's institutions of higher education and increasingly across its K-12 schools as well.

Even when the Department of Education has initiated actions against institutions of higher learning that have tolerated, and often supported, anti-Jewish practices on campus, its interventions have usually been nothing more than slaps on the wrist which have brought little change in the behavior of the targeted institutions. An example is the DOE's handling of a 2019 Title VI complaint against the University of North Carolina at Chapel Hill. In the wake of the complaint, the university struck an agreement with the DOE, but it apparently failed to comply with its obligations under the agreement. The DOE had to open a new Title VI investigation of the university in late 2023.[3]

Moreover, other arms of the federal government also have a capacity to enforce anti-bigotry laws and push aggressively against violators but have yet to be enlisted in the struggle to address anti-Jewish bias. Instead, federal laws are routinely flouted in the treatment of Jews at all education levels.

---

3   Andrew Lapin, "Feds to Probe University of North Carolina's Response to Harsh Anti-Israel Episode," Jewish Telegraphic Agency, December 27, 2023.

With regard to state agencies, Departments of Education in states that have adopted the International Holocaust Remembrance Alliance (IHRA) definition of antisemitism can inform school district heads and college and university presidents about the IHRA definition and its implications for their domains. They can also train teachers in applying the IHRA definition as a compulsory part of "cultural competencies" training for teacher licensing. In every state, Education Department officials can do site visits to schools at which there have been problems in dealing with antisemitism.

Another area of potential government action against the promotion of anti-semitism and antizionism is enforcement of the Federal Agents Registration Act (FARA), which requires persons or entities that lobby for foreign governments, organizations, or individuals to register with the Department of Justice and describe their relationship to their foreign funders, their activities, and their remuneration. FARA's aim is transparency vis-à-vis foreign efforts to influence domestic opinion and government policies. Enforcement of FARA is typically lax, and its requirements are often violated.

For example, members of Congress have fought an uphill battle to have the Department of Justice (DOJ) force Al Jazeera to register as an agent of Qatar. This media organization operates as a mouthpiece of the Qatari government, including in its promotion of the Muslim Brotherhood, Hamas, Hezbollah, and other terror entities, and in its anti-Israel and anti-Jewish propaganda. The Justice Department in 2020 finally ordered Al Jazeera to register, but five years later it still has not done so and the DOJ has done little to force compliance.[4] The DOJ has acted against some individual Americans employed as agents of Qatar who failed to register under FARA. It can clearly do much more.

As noted in an earlier chapter, Qatar is the largest foreign financier of American institutions of higher education. Its money has bought anti-Jewish and anti-Israel indoctrination on campuses and, via dissemination of campus-designed curricula, in grade schools as well. Other foreign entities have also contributed to advancing, among other objectives, an anti-Israel and anti-Jewish agenda in American academia. The federal government could be doing much more, via FARA, to render such efforts more transparent and enlighten the American public about this significant source of the rising anti-Jewish and antizionist bigotry.

---

4   See, for example, Josh Boswell, "News Channel Al Jazeera is Slammed for 'Flouting' Government Orders to Register as a Foreign Agent of Qatar, New Report Finds," *Daily Mail*, March 22, 2023.

But to get federal and state governments to do more to fight against anti-Jewish bias in grade schools and in higher education, against BDS efforts, and against foreign underwriting of the assault on American Jews, American Jews and their allies need to push for such greater action, both directly and through their representatives. There has been some such prodding, but again it has typically come not from major organizations but rather from smaller Jewish groups. In addition, those efforts have at times been opposed by major organizations as, for example, in the ADL's opposition to passage of anti-BDS legislation.

Individuals in the community can, of course, also push for greater government action. They can write and call their elected representatives to express their outrage over the antisemitism promoted by various sources including elements of the Democrat Party. And they can forcefully urge greater government employment of the tools at its disposal to roll back the assault on American Jews.

More on the Anti-Israel Element within Mainstream Jewish Institutions

The failure of various mainstream Jewish institutions, including large legacy institutions, to address the antisemitism coming from sources other than the Far Right, even at times voicing support for non-Far Right purveyors of antisemitism, is reflected in the recurrent criticisms of Israel expressed by these Jewish institutions. They choose to understand the hatred promoted by the groups with which they feel some affinity, hatred which almost invariably has an anti-Israel and antizionist component, as primarily aimed at Israel, and they then join in criticizing the Jewish state. They do so to underscore their connectedness with those groups and to exempt themselves—or to reinforce the delusion that they are exempted—from those groups' anti-Jewish hate. In their expressions of criticisms of Israel, these mainstream Jewish voices come closest to the extremist rhetoric of "Jewish" groups like Jewish Voice for Peace and IfNotNow, which embrace, and join forces with, those seeking the annihilation of Israel.

The depth of this rot—about which most American Jews know little, but of which all who care about the American Jewish community and Israel should be aware—was anecdotally addressed in a 2022 article by Daniel Gordis, a founder of, and Koret distinguished fellow at, Shalem College in Jerusalem.[5] Gordis noted that, a few weeks before writing the piece, he had read a Facebook post that talked of a recent controversy surrounding Avodah, a Jewish organization founded in 1998 and dedicated to sponsoring programs aimed at "promoting social and economic justice in our communities and in America." The post reported that Avodah had hired for a social media position and then let go someone who was discovered to have put out a number of tweets attacking Zionists as "genocidal freaks," "extremely ugly," and more in the same vein. Subsequently, some 150-plus alumni of Avodah programs condemned the organization for firing the person, characterized the firing as a violation of proper openness to diverse viewpoints on Israel, and called on the organization to make amends for its decision and pay compensation to its ex-employee.

The author of the Facebook post thought this attack on Avodah, like the tweets of the fired employee, was sickening and beyond the pale. Gordis agrees:

> What I've come to understand during [recent weeks spent in the United States], that I realize I didn't fully understand prior, is just how mainstream anti-Zionism has become in many [Jewish] circles here. Someone shared with me a letter sent recently to a leading American rabbi, complaining that this rabbi's congregation had had a guest speaker who derided anti-Zionists. The complaint was that the speaker had no right to characterize anti-Zionists in a negative light. The letter read in part: All of us think anti-Zionist Jews deserve a place in this shul and deserve not to be demonized or called antisemitic... Many of them are young adults or teenagers who represent the future of the synagogue and the Jewish community . . . They are self-loving, community-loving Jews who also believe that the safest, most just, most moral future for Israel and Palestine ensures all Israelis and Palestinians have equal rights.

Gordis goes on:

> Let's leave aside the utter inanity of the notion that the end of Zionism would guarantee a "safe" future for the Jews of the

---

5   Daniel Gordis, "On Anti-Zionism, Idolatry and Adultery," Substack, July 26, 2022.

region. One has to be willfully ignorant of both Jewish history and the dynamics of the Middle East to imagine any such scenario . . .

What most struck me about this letter was the confidence of the writers, the sense that there was no reason to be meek when they told their rabbi that they are proud anti-Zionists. Theirs is not some marginal synagogue like Tzedek Chicago . . . which made waves earlier this year when it announced that anti-Zionism is a "core value" of their congregation. No, this is a major, nationally recognized and rightly admired flagship congregation. But still, there was no shame, no sense on the part of the proud anti-Zionists that theirs is a position on the margins of Jewish life.

I've also been meeting with some rabbinical students while I'm here. They go to all kinds of schools on both coasts, and are from all over the country. What have they wanted to speak about? They want to share how hard it is to be a Zionist in rabbinical school today. They want to talk about how most of their classmates self-define either as "non-Zionists" or "anti-Zionists" and how they, the Zionists, are worried that they're going to lose friends and (get this . . .) possibly lose jobs if they continue to make it known that they endorse the idea of a Jewish state (even if they're critical of many of its policies, as are many Israelis).

Those shamelessly defending or promoting antizionism within the Jewish community, such as those Gordis referenced above, insist they are committed Jews, concerned about the future of the Jewish people. But, as Gordis notes at one point, "To actively campaign against the state which will soon be home to the majority of your people, thus rendering them vulnerable in myriad ways, is a strange way to love the Jewish people." And it is a very peculiar love that would withhold from your own people the right of self-determination in their ancestral home while believing it a natural right of other peoples.

But, of course, their antizionism and hostility towards Israel have nothing to do with concerns about the well-being of the Jewish people. Rather, it has everything to do with these individuals' concerns about their own well-being. It has to do with the wishful delusions they share with those leaders of Jewish institutions and organizations who are silent in the face of all but Far Right antisemitism and make no mention of the antisemitism coming from those parts of the wider population with which they choose to identify. It has to do with wanting to believe that only Israel and Zionism are the object of hatred from these groups, and that by ignoring it, giving some legitimacy to it, or joining in full-throated support for its attacks on Israel, they will assure their own exemption from the hatred.

Gordis, perhaps because he is more attuned to what is going on in the synagogues and seminaries than in other American Jewish institutions, is more attuned to the failures there; and there are major failures there, as noted in the previous chapter. He writes, "A huge part of the problem lies in the rabbinical schools, of all sorts, which today have become wellsprings of non- and anti-Zionism . . . [S]uffice it to say that we need rabbinical schools where anti- or even non-Zionism are considered far beyond the pale." Gordis points out that there are social and religious views—he lists several—that, if espoused by an applicant, would very likely get him or her rejected by seminaries:

> It's just that when it comes to Israel, anything is fair game. . . . No one can stop anyone from wishing the state did not exist. But we could stop them from being admitted to rabbinical schools. We could create a community where they would blush before writing to their rabbi that they're anti-Zionists. We could make this as sacred a Jewish principle as some of the others [he had mentioned earlier.] . . . The real test we face is whether anything at all is still sacred, still inviolable . . . And if it's not, the question becomes not whether we'll survive, but whether we deserve to.

Perhaps; but even that question becomes moot. Because, again, American Jews are a primary target of the rising antisemitism in America from all sources. As noted at the end of the previous chapter, the demise of the Jews, and not simply a distancing from Israel, will be the logical ultimate step, the *reductio ad absurdum*, should nothing be inviolable; should the increasingly more entrenched, potentially dominant priority within the community become the Jewish accommodation of anti-Jewish sentiment.

But there is a particular dark irony in the fact that Jewish educators, in seminaries and on college and university campuses, distance themselves from, or outright attack, the Zionist project and push for its demise; a dark irony even beyond the threat their doing so poses to half of world Jewry and the almost certain negative ramifications for the other half.

The Jewish *resorgimento*, the national rebirth of the Jewish people, its articulated aspirations, and the history of its efforts to realize those aspirations, when honestly told, have been and continue to be an inspiration for much of mankind. Israel's story has been and continues to be an inspiration and a model perhaps most notably for those who, as members of victimized communities, have yet to achieve their own communal self-determination. It also has provided and continues to provide a compelling, motivating example for communities that have taken the first steps towards self-determination but face daunting difficulties in the quest to transform their young polities into free, safe, and prosperous homelands for their people.

How ironic then that, in the face of the hatred directed against both Diaspora Jews and Israel, Jewish educators in large numbers—typically social justice warriors in their own minds—target Israel, embrace the antizionist calumnies of the haters, and join the ranks of their supporters and fellow travelers. But such betrayals have always been characteristic of minorities under siege. For those not broken by the siege, who are armed by nurturing education and steadfast upbringing or by their own iron integrity, the task is to become themselves not only resistors but educators. The alternative, however disguised in claims of higher principle, is an ignoble capitulation to murderous bigotry, which serves only to advance the world-diminishing campaign for hatred's victory.

Bibliography

Aschheim, Steven E. *Brothers and Strangers: The East European Jew in German and German-Jewish Consciousness.* Cambridge. MA: Harvard University Press, 1976.

Ben-Horin, Meir. *Max Nordau, Philosopher of Human Solidarity.* New York: Conference of Jewish Social Studies, 1956.

Ben-Sasson, H. H., ed. *A History of the Jewish People.* Cambridge, MA: Harvard University Press, 1976.

Berlin, Isaiah. *Karl Marx: His Life and Environment.* Oxford: Oxford University Press, 1978.

Bernstein, David L. *Woke Antisemitism.* New York: Wicked Son, 2022.

Brandeis, Louis D. *Brandeis on Zionism: A Collection of Addresses and Statements by Louis D. Brandeis.* Washington, D.C.: Zionist Organization of America, 1942.

Brenner, Joseph Hayyim. "Self-Criticism." In *The Zionist Idea,* edited by Arthur Hertzberg, 307–312. New York: Harper and Row, 1959.

Chabon, Michael, and Ayelet Waldman, ed. *Kingdom of Olives and Ash: Writers Confront the Occupation.* New York: Harper Perennial, 2017.

Connerton, Paul. *The Tragedy of Enlightenment: An Essay on the Frankfurt School.* New York: Cambridge University Press, 1980.

Dawidowicz, Lucy. *What is the Use of Jewish History?* New York: Schocken, 1992.

Fioktistov, Ilya. *Terror in the Cradle of Liberty: How Boston Became a Center for Islamic Extremism.* New York: Encounter Books, 2019.

Freud, Anna. *The Ego and the Mechanisms of Defense.* Madison, CT: International Universities Press, 1966. (First published London: Hogarth, 1936.)

"Gabriel Riesser." *Encyclopedia Judaica*, vol. 14, 166–169. Jerusalem: Ketem Publishing, 1972.

Gates, Henry Louis, Jr. "Black Demagogues and Pseudo-Scholars." *The New York Times*, July 20, 1992.

———. "The New Black Anti-Semitism is Top-Down and Dangerous." *The Baltimore Sun*, July 22, 1992.

Gilman, Sander L. *Jewish Self-Hatred.* Baltimore, MD: Johns Hopkins, 1986.

Goren, Arthur A., ed. *Dissenter in Zion: From the Writings of Judah L. Magnes.* Cambridge, MA: Harvard University Press, 1982.

Hazony, Yoram. *The Jewish State.* New York: Basic Books, 2000.

Hertzberg, Arthur, ed. *The Zionist Idea.* New York: Harper, 1959.

———. *The Jews in America.* New York: Columbia University Press, 1997.

Herzl, Theodor. *The Jewish State.* New York: Dover, 1988.

Jacobs, Charles, and Avi Goldwasser, eds. *Betrayal.* New York: Wicked Son, 2023.

Karsh, Efraim. *Arafat's War.* New York: Grove Press, 2003.

Kuntzel, Mattias. *Jihad and Jew-Hatred.* Candor, NY: Telos Press, 2009.

Lessing, Theodor. *Einmal und Nie Wieder.* Guetersloh: Bertelsmann Sachbuchverlag, 1969.

———. *Der Judische Selbsthass.* Munich: Matthes and Seitz Verlag, 1984.

Levin, Kenneth. *The Oslo Syndrome: Delusions of a People under Siege.* Hanover, NH: Smith and Kraus Global, 2005.

———. *Unconscious Fantasy in Psychotherapy.* Northvale, NJ: Jason Aronson, 1993.

Lewin, Kurt. *Resolving Social Conflicts.* New York: Harper, 1948.

Lewis, Bernard. *Semites and Anti-Semites.* New York: W. W. Norton, 1986.

Lipset, Seymour Martin, and Earl Raab. *Jews and the New American Scene.* Cambridge, MA: Harvard University Press, 1995.

Lipstadt, Deborah. *Beyond Belief.* New York: Free Press, 1986.

Liptzin, Solomon. *Germany's Stepchildren*. Cleveland: Meridian, 1961.

Manuel, Frank E. *A Requiem for Karl Marx*. Cambridge, MA: Harvard University Press, 1995.

Marx, Karl. *Early Writings*. Translated and edited by T. B. Bottomore. New York: McGraw-Hill, 1964.

Medoff, Rafael. *The Deafening Silence*. New York: Shapolsky, 1987.

Meyer, Michael A. *The Origins of the Modern Jew*. Detroit, MI: Wayne State University Press, 1967.

Morse, Arthur D. *While Six Million Died*. New York: Random House, 1967.

"Near East and South Asia, Daily Report Supplement, Israel-PLO Agreement." Foreign Broadcast Information Service, Tuesday, September 14, 1993, 4–5.

Rosenblatt, Gary, "Frustration with Israel is Growing Here at Home." *New York Jewish Week*, January 6, 2016.

Rubin, Barry. *Assimilation and Its Discontents*. New York: Times Books, 1995.

Schorsch, Ismar. *From Text to Context: The Turn to History in Modern Judaism*. Hanover, NH: Brandeis University Press, 1994.

Steel, Ronald. *Walter Lippmann and the American Century*. Boston, MA: Little, Brown, 1980.

Stotsky, Steven. *Indoctrinating Our Youth: How a U.S. Public School Curriculum Skews the Arab-Israeli Conflict and Islam*. Boston, MA: Committee for Accuracy in Middle East Reporting in America, 2017.

Talese, Gay. *The Kingdom and the Power*. New York: World, 1966.

Teveth, Shabtai. *Ben-Gurion: The Burning Ground*. Boston, MA: Houghton, Mifflin, 1987.

Weininger, Otto. *Sex and Character*. New York: Howard Fertig, 2003.

Wistrich, Robert S. *The Jews of Vienna in the Age of Franz Joseph*. Oxford: Littman Library, 1989.

———. *Muslim Anti-Semitism: A Clear and Present Danger*. New York: American Jewish Committee, 2002.

———. *Revolutionary Jews from Marx to Trotsky*. New York: Harper and Row, 1976.

Wyman, David S. *The Abandonment of the Jews*. New York: Pantheon, 1984.

Zohn, Harry. *Karl Kraus*. New York: Twayne, 1971.

Index

Vanderbilt University, 122
Vienna, 50, 52

Waldman, Ayelet, 137
Wall. *See* Western Wall
Wall Street Journal, The, 29
Wallenberg, Raoul, 80–81
Warburg, Felix, 101–3, 111
War on Poverty, 84
War Refugee Board (WRB), 79–82
Warsaw, 75
Washington, D.C., 27, 154
Washington, Joshua, 19n12
Washington Examiner, The, journal, 16n6
Washington Free Beacon, website, 1, 17n8
Washington Post, The, 7
Waterloo, 68
Weinberg, Andrew, 88n18
Weininger, Otto, 52–54
Wertheimer, Jack, 84n13
West Bank, 39, 90, 92, 107–9, 125–26, 130, 133–34, 143
West/ Western countries, 1–2, 13, 17, 21–23, 43, 59, 62, 66, 72, 75, 88, 103, 120–21
Western Wall (in Jerusalem), 127–28
West Point, military academy, 121
White Paper, immigration limiting document, 103
white supremacists, 6, 13, 20–21, 23, 25–28, 35, 44, 150

Wiesenthal Center, 88m18
Wines, Michael, 91n22
Wise, Stephen S., rabbi, 78, 82, 101
Wistrich, Robert S., 52n9, 54, 73n33, 73n35, 74n36, 87
White House, 95, 107
Women's March protests, 36
World War I, 56, 78, 100
World War II, 23, 83–84, 111
Wyman, David S., 80n3

X, Malcolm, 25
X. *See* Twitter

Yale, 141–42
Yalies4Palestine, group, 141
Yazidis, religious group, 132
Yemen, 132
Yiddish language, 34, 48–50, 68
Yishuv, community, 77, 102–4
Ynet News, website, 17n8
Yom Kippur War (1973), 32

Zaray, Morin, 138n65
Zionism/Zionist, 10, 15, 30n4, 33, 35n7, 42, 44, 46, 47n1, 54, 56, 75–79, 82, 90, 98–104, 111, 114, 135n56, 139, 142, 149, 151, 160, 164–66
Zohn, Harry, 50n7, 51n8

www.ingramcontent.com/pod-product-compliance
Lightning Source LLC
Chambersburg PA
CBHW071951260326
41914CB00004B/791